the internet
now in handy book form

First published in Great Britain in 2007 by
Portico Books
10 Southcombe Street
London
W14 0RA

An imprint of Anova Books Company Ltd.

ISBN 1 90603 200 9

A CIP catalogue record for this book is available from the British Library.

10 9 8 7 6 5 4 3 2 1

Printed and bound by Mondadori, Toledo, Spain.

This book can be ordered direct from the publisher.
Contact the marketing department, but try your bookshop first.

www.anovabooks.com

the internet
now in handy book form

david mccandless

PORTICO

written, designed and illustrated by

David McCandless

tag: writers

Kesta Desmond Piers Gibbon Aegir Hallmundir Steve Hill Rhodri Marsden Toby Slater
Phil South

tag: additional material

Nick Farnhill Damon Green Lisa James Paul Lakin Duncan MacDonald Joel Morris (for "Cocoon For Men") Alex
Morris Nik Roope James Robinson Iain Tait Anne Marie-Payne Doc Sleaze Dave Walker

tag: illustrations

Chris Ahchay Peter Ayres John Comeau Elliot Elam Hnldesign Kanzune Dean Kerrigan Noah Leininger
Mathemagician Matt Simon Pegg Lee Robinson Neurozys Nik Roope Phil South Simon A. Sheridan Schwenz David Sullivan
Miles Tudor Doctor When and Alex Morris

tag: cover design

Nicky Gibson

tag: additional design

Mark Beach Delfina Bottesini David Martin Marc Davies Steve 'Buzz 'Pearce Lassi
Lammassaari Aegir Hallmundir Vici MacDonald

tag: production

Golden Cockerel Book Design

tag: submitted photos

Craig Bonney, Colin Cooper, Janine Hall, Michelle McCandless, Natasha Morabito, Priscilla Moura, Laura Price,
Kathryn Ruch, Kirsty Stephenson, Duncan Swain, Miles Tudor, Emily Wells, Kier Young.

tag: special thanks

Tom Bromley, Charlie Brooker, Laura Brudenell, Light Club, Hana Cree, Kesta Desmond, Elizabeth Dunn, Nick
Farnhill, Piers Gibbon, Holly McCandless-Desmond, Helen Ponting, Laura Price, Toby Slater, Simon Trewin and
istockphoto.com.

tag: links

for weblinks for all these talented people see page 138

Welcome To The Future...

Welcome To The Internet:

Congratulations. You are now the proud owner of the future. These pages will take you through setting up your book, readying your viewing apparatus and using the main features of the book. Enjoy!

text

image

spine   cover

TOP TIP: Stay Online!
When reading try to keep your eyes on the lines or 'online' to use the correct Internet terminology. This will help download the sense of the sentence to your mind.

TOP TIP: Hands Up!
Order your Handsfree device and a range of exciting accessories to improve your book experience. See page 136.

How this Book Works

This book uses magic particles - called photons - to transmit text and image information stored on 'pages' into your eyes. Your eyes then send these patterns down a magic tunnel to your brain which reconstructs the images in full 3D.

How To Read This Book

Here are our tips for best use:
1) Hold your book in a relaxed pose.
2) Keep the pages at least 20 cms from your face at all times.
3) Use the arrow on the spine to orientate the correct direction.
4) Two handed use is also permissable but watch out for objects ahead of you.
5) Try to use clean hands as dirt and grime and bodily fluids may impair performance of this device.
Now smile and enjoy the ride!

Please note: the quality and depth of your viewing experience depends on many factors: brain quality, thought width, processing speed etc. We recommend that users upgrade to the latest brain hardware whenever possible.

WARNING

Never use this book in a vehicle while driving unless you are using a handsfree device such as another person or an official *The Internet Now In Handy Book Form!* handsfree device. If you don't have a handsfree device, stop, park your car safely and turn the engine off before opening your book. Never park on a motorway slip road or the hard shoulder unless it is an emergency. You could die a cheap and humiliating death.

Problems?

If your book is malfunctioning in some way, or you're just not "getting it", try closing, waiting five seconds and then opening the book again. This usually clears up most problems. If that doesn't work, try having a nice cup of tea and a lie down. See if that helps. If not, pop a Valium and maybe get a madam to swaddle your head in hot towels for half an hour. Usually works for us. Or you can visit our Technical Support department at the back of the book. They'll be overjoyed to help you.

Now In Handy Book Form

Get Interacting! This book is a full non-linear bi-directional interactive experience. That means you can go to any website, whenever you like, basically, at the swish of a page. Allow us to explain how...

Page Turn™

PageTurn™ is an exciting new technology that provides Internet style interactivity in handy book form. Many of the links on the pages are 'live' and denoted by a PageTurn™ symbols like these:

When you see PageTurn™ links like these, PageTurn™ to the PageTurn™ page indicated.

How To PageTurn™

1. Grasp an outside corner of the page with your thumb and forefinger.

2. Pull the page upwards and away from you in a single motion.

3. Drop the page on the other side of the spine.

Other ways to interact

Meet The Avatars

Avatars are real people - chosen by a person with a degree in demographics, to represent the typical people found on the Internet. Many have their own webpages in the book and - watch out! - their own opinions. There's someone for everyone! ▶010

Please note: any views expressed by the Avatars are their own and do not represent the views of the Bahoogle Corporation or any of its satellite corporations.

Homepage

If you're already an experienced book user, you can go right ahead and start browsing this exciting online world. Why not try our homepage as a starting point for exploring the great services and exciting free content this book offers... ▶008

Please note: the Bahoogle Corporation is not responsible for any offence, laughter or shame caused by the content of this book.

Connect with other book users using 'wifi'

Yes, this book is fully compatible with the latest forms of wireless technology also known as 'wifi'. This functionality however is still at the prototype stage. Performance may be unstable or even absent. In the future we hope to upgrade this facility. Until then, you may find and connect with other users using this simple process. Close the book and wave it above your head while shouting 'wop wop wop'. Alternatively make a scanning noise, like a periscope or a Geiger counter, and follow the book to whoever responds.

Please note: The Bahoogle Corporation cannot take responsibility for any damage to property, personal health or social standing resulting from the use of this feature.

PLEASE REGISTER YOUR COPY OF THE INTERNET: NOW IN HANDY BOOK FORM! ▶133

It won't actually protect it from theft. Or allow us to replace your copy should it go astray. But do it anyway, eh?

THE INTERNET

Featured **Entertainment** **Sports** **Life**

National Hypochondriacs Service

Got a headache? Slightly dry mouth? Dry lips? Sounds like viral meningitis. Or SARS. Or Ebola. Or all three.

More amateurish self-diagnosis ▶054

HackersDIY
Let's make a harrier jump jet out of an old piano, some wires and a pair of nail clippers.
▶100

Meme Museum
The best email send-arounds ever archived in one place for you to um, send around.
▶111

Internet Alert
Don't fall foul of spam, viruses, trojans, scams, infectoids, downloadits and fakes.
▶102

Drug Alert!
Protect your children from the world's No.3 most deadly threat.
▶024

THE F* & C***
Beer In The Morning Noon And Night**
The best pubs and the best beer and the best fights - all reviewed.
▶036

JustBYou
Make-up. Chocolate. Men. Yoga. Keep up with all the things that matter. Girls only!
▶044

Interact

Tech

gadgets   **high quality gadgets**   **software**

COCOON FOR MEN   **Schmapple**   **amasszone**
▶030   ▶022   ▶070

People

Our Beautiful Wedding

Lucky lovebirds Darren and Emma beat over three other newly weds to win a place for their wedding in this interactive book thing.

Find out how it went ▶023

personals with **poormatch**.com

masterfulcock69
I am a dominant and skilled lover. I looking for someone with low self-esteem to practice on.
▶026

Cath
Hi! I'm Cath as in "Catholic". My dad's a priest and that's why he named me that.
▶028

Widower
37 year old man with GSOH seeks blonde, alive replacement for dead, blonde wife.
▶027

Schizoid
I'm told, by myself, that I'm a good person to know and we think that's bang on. Don't we?
▶025

Blogs

Tune into the drone of the Blogosphere
Our top diarists are university-trained in narcissism. They're paid to turn the banal foam that forms on the surface of their minds into miles and miles of opinionated waffle.

THE DULLEST BLOG IN THE WORLD ▶083

ecologic.al ▶041   **spodwire** ▶098

Parentingsureisfun.com ▶060

Getting Out

Modern Adventure Days

Pampering. Adventure. Luxury. Ever wanted to experience the height of life? Just pay a largeish sum of money and for 24 hours you can have a taste of the Dolce Vita. Then you can piss off. ▶126

Pop Up Ads

Pop Up Ads

Not got enough pop up ads in your life? Want more pop up ads? Ever wondered what it'd be like to have more pop up ads?
Well, now you can. ▶086 ▶050 ▶114 ▶120

NOW IN HANDY BOOK FORM!

Our sites

Preserver Limited ▶068

Bullies Reunion ▶058

 .com ▶079

hamstrjobs.com ▶056

mineminemyplace
a place for yourself and no one else ▶087

 ▶043

🌐 BOLLOXPEDIA ▶065

🌐 CHINAPEDIA ▶069

R E A L
LIFE an amazing 3D world
now with over six
billion residents
▶034

Sportobix ▶042
sport for those who don't do any

**AMERICA'S MOST
WANTED VACATIONS** ▶093

Entertainment

 Tranquillise Yourself With Triviality
Kill hours of your valuable life watching hilarious
clips of kittens falling off washing machines.

UFOs - truly science
fiction? Pageturn to
find out
07:07 ▶038

Totally gruesome and
totally funny!
Pageturn to watch!
02:18 ▶039

Night vision footage
purporting to be
something. Pageturn
to find out what ▶040

 **Gossip? Gossip** ▶097
The latest unsurprising and
untitillating hearsay you already knew.

More Bloody Personals

 the hi-tech way to find, meet
and have other people

 MAGICK DATING ▶064
MIDDLE WORLD'S PREMIERE PERSONALS SERVICE

Buy!

📕 Buy books	▶029
🏠 Buy houses	▶037
🍿 Buy food	▶051
Buy merchandise	▶136

**Buy back
issues** of this
cool Net Book
▶134

Grot

THE DARK NET
dare you...?
▶118

Meet The Avatars

The Internet's not just about wires, pipes and other digital flimflam. It's also about people. Real people with blood and everything!

Katherine Merchant, CEO

Leader and change agent
I'm glamorous, intelligent, creative and successful with a big heart and an even bigger house.
Want to employ me? ▶ 057
Want to sleep with me? ▶ 028

Darren & Emma

Our Wedding
We won a national competition to have our beautiful perfect wedding documented in this incredible book. So exciting!!! Start finding all about us right now! ▶ 023

N@v3IG@z0R

Check our my galleries
Hey. What to say? I'm into blogging, picture-sharing and laptopping everything in my life. And I'm 99 years old BTW all you creepy f**ks who keep emailing . ▶ 092

Colonic

Perfection Is Not A Myth
Today's workout: 8 lateral rises; 20 press ups; 25 lunges; 2 x 10 upright rows; 3 mins of self doubt; quick winegum binge; masturbate; bed.
▶ 105

Tokyo Ritz

Ciao!
The Vamp Tramp. The Heiress With The Mostest. In exchange for heavy cross promotion of my ailing first album, I've agreed to host my mineminemyplace page in this book.
▶ 089

BloodyWomen

What?
I love women as long as they're naked and tonguing each other. I'm the curator of the 'dark pages' of this book. ▶ 115

Writer

Louche is the pen scribing this intro
An even keel is all I ask for, truly, but instead scatterings of words on a chalk white page. Is this all I am? I muse, a deep one, with a vibrating menstrual bass. Date me. ▶028

Mark & Sue

Perfect Parents
We have over ten beautiful healthy children and a lovely big house next to the best school in the world. We're friendly, outgoing, rich and alive. Read our nauseating blog. ▶060

Sophia From Arabia

Message Me!
I'm Sophia from Arabia or somewhere very similar. Hi everybody! I've studied English sinse Autumn. It's very! I want like to meet habndsome guys and gays to practice my French. Kisses! You gotta laugh! ▶064

Johnathon

This kerning is two picas off
Anyway my name is Caleb. I am 28. I am a senior POV admin at Bolloxpedia and spend my spare time roving Bahoogle Earth for cock-shaped geological abnormalities. ▶048

Hassel Davidoff

Do I need to describe myself?
Didn't think so. ▶067

You?

Would you like to appear in a book?
Fancy being famous? Bet you do. Visit the electronic version of this book here. ▶105

IMPORTANT
Licence Agreement

PLEASE READ THIS CONTRACT CAREFULLY

By opening this book you and Bahoogle.com agree to be bound by the terms and conditions set out on this page. You may want to take time to read and consider them before you proceed.

By turning the page you accept all the terms and conditions of this non-negotiated agreement, ("THE UNBELIEVEMENT") including the most facistic ones. You agree that this agreement is enforceable against you, your family and any living sentient entity who has touched this book. "Book" means this book. "You" means you. Got that? Good. Shall we continue? Yeah. Thought so.

Oh and we reserve the right to modify this agreement at any time without telling you but expect you to be fully bound to it.

SPECIFIC CLAUSES

Services
This book is licensed for use on the Bahoogle network only. Use on another (inferior) networks constitutes a breach of license. This is considered a serious crime. The only appropriate punishment is death.

Copyright
All the content of this book is copyright to The Bahoogle Corporation forever. It is, however, grudgingly, licensed to you under a 'fair use' contract. See the terms on the page opposite.

If you can't be arsed to read it, here is a summary. You may quote the content in this book once, and once only, near a watercooler (or other social focal point) for example. This constitutes "fair use" of this material. However, further use of this material - for example, repeating it to friends or reading it out in public to two or more people - requires legal permission, a special licence and subscription fee payable to the Bahoogle Corporation Ltd.

Use without a license consitutes an severe infringement of copyright under the Digital Millenial Strangulation Of Internet Act Bill (2005). Such infringement is punishable by death.

Rights of use
You may read this book with one or both of your eyes. If anyone else's eyes are used, a licence fee is due. Multiple eye use without license is considered a crime. The penalty? Death.

Back up copy
You may obtain your one backup copy by buying another copy of The Internet Now In Handy Book Form provided it is only read by you. Making your own backup copy is strictly illegal. If caught, you will be put to death. It's the only language you goddamn drones understand.

Modification
You may not customize, write on, extend the functionality of the book other than in the allocated 'interactive areas'. Infringement of this stipulation is a crime. What is the punishment, you ask? Do we have to say?

Suspension of services
We may suspend some or all of the Services you use without giving you notice if:
– you do not laugh enough
– you laugh too much in an annoying fashion, such as braying or smutty chuckles or a low hacking puke-like laugh like a cat with a pencil in its throat
– we have good reason to believe your book is being used for improper purposes, such as propping up a wonky table, given as a snap gift to a far-flung relative, or used as the switch to a secret passageway behind the bookcase.

Worldwide roaming services
Should work in other countries, but Bahoogle are not responsible for any misunderstanding or violence that might incur from use of the book and its content in foreign climes.

Your rights to terminate the contract
You may terminate this contract at any time by throwing the book in the bin, dumping it in the attic, letting a friend 'borrow it' and then forgetting about it, selling it on kakbay, or letting it drop behind a sofa / radiator / bookcase.

Liability

Though we have licensed and host these pages for profit and the sole exploitation of your wallet (though we make a big song and dance about 'community' and how 'wow' it all is), the Bahoogle Corporation cannot be held responsible for any of the content herein. In legalese: BAHOOGLE.COM MAKES NO WARRANTIES, CONDITIONS, INDEMNITIES, REPRESENTATIONS, SHADOW PUPPETS, HALF TRUTHS, LIES (EXPRESS, IMPLIED, WHISPERED OR WHIMPERED), WHETHER BY STATUTE, COMMON LAW, CUSTOM USAGE OR OTHERWISE, FOR ANY CONTENT FOUND IN THIS GODDAMNED BOOK ALREADY.

Indemnity

YOU AGREE TO HOLD BAHOOGLE AND ANY APPLICABLE SERVICE PROVIDER HARMLESS FROM ANY AND ALL LIABILITIES, LOSSES, ACTIONS, DAMAGES, RIBCAGE SPLITTAGE, SOILED UNDERWEAR, SPILT FOOD, SPAT OUT COFFEE OR ANY CLAIMS (INCLUDING ALL REASONABLE EXPENSES, COSTS, AND ATTORNEYS FEES) ARISING OUT OF OR RELATING TO ANY USE OF, OR RELIANCE ON, THIS BOOK FOR ENTERTAINMENT AND HUMOUR WITHOUT LIMITATION FOREVER AND EVER AMEN. TURN AROUND, TOUCH THE GROUND, BAGSIE NOT IT.

Further more

AS LONG AS WE CONTINUE TO SHOUT AT YOU IN CAPITALS AND USE EXTREMELY CIRCUMLOCUTIONS VERBIAGE, YOU AGREE TO GLAZE OVER AND SCAN THE PARAGRAPH, BARELY RETAINING ITS MEANING, COMPLETELY NOT GIVING A SHIT, STARING AT THIS PAGE BUT REALLY BEHIND IT INTO YOUR OWN THOUGHTS UNTIL WE GET DOWN TO THE BOTTOM SOMEWHERE AND WE SUDDENLY SAY "DO YOU AGREE?" WHICH WILL CAUSE (A) YOU TO JUMP SUDDENLY IN YOUR CHAIR; (B) THE DAYDREAM OF YOU BEING A SORT OF WEREWOLF THAT COULD TAKE PART IN MYSTERIES AND SOLVE CRIME (BUT ONLY AT NIGHT) TO DISSIPATE.

Sign Here

_____

Print Name

_____

Did you sign it?

You didn't did you?

Go back. Go on.

Don't make us get our CAPITALS OUT.

OMFG   I Swear   If   I Have   To Look   **At Another »**

I'm going: ⦿ to climb   ◯ the nearest water tower

[stupid] [goddamn webpage]

With! A high powered sniper rifle.

I've Had Enough - Of This Overgrown - Electronic - Shopping Mall - And Its Huge Porn Section

© Just check my email one last time

Bahoogle
YOUR HOMEPAGE

Bahoogle Good News

World Peace Sparks Outpourings Of Joy ▶017

Black Forest To Be Made Out Of Chocolate by 2030 ▶017

Penis size "no advantage in sex" Dutch study finds ▶017

TODAY'S LUCKY COLOUR

Puce
Today it's puce

TheTruthTheTruthTheTruth.com

Case 45, Section III, Appendix 9, Footnote 3
"THE CIGAR-SHAPED OBJECT"
NOT A DECADE GOES BY WITHOUT SOME EERIE CIGAR-SHAPED OBJECT APPEARING ON A NASSA DEEP SPACE PHOTOGRAPH. IS THIS EVIDENCE OF SUPER PARANORMAL INTELLIGENCES DWARFING OUR OWN DEVELOPING CIGAR-SHAPED TECHNOLOGIES TO EXPLORE THE UNIVERSE OR JUST BITS OF DUST ON THE LENS AS THE "ESTABLISHMENT" WOULD HAVE US BELIEVE. Read no more ▶108

Fat Person In Really Bad Jumper

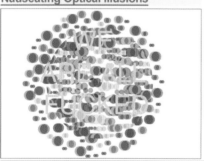

«   »

(c) Nassa

Nauseating Optical Illusions

Mindless Trivia Daily   edit

Today is National Buboe Day in Japan. Large groups throw beans and plums at temple doors to drive away bacteria. It doesn't work.
more at bolloxpedia.org ▶065

Hippy Quote of The Day   edit

"It's like...we're all one, big, brain... you, me, shimmering, each of us in a brain cell in a massive global ubermind in shock at realising its is-ness." Terrence McKennot
more of this mulch at narcorati ▶124

Meme Of The Day.com

Remember the Squillion Dollar Homepage?
the mememuseum ▶111

NeoDictionary   edit

schlepilepsy \ sh-lep-uh-lep-see \ *adjective*
Being prone to fits when a far-away friend requests you to visit them. "I only asked her to come to South London but she had a complete schlepileptic fit."

Hubble Endescope Daily Image

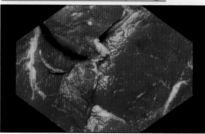

buy the book today at amasszone.com ▶029

New streetdrug of the day

Incredulosity Anti-stroke drug found to cause short term memory loss and wide-eyed surprise
Side effects: sexual exploitation
Duration: 8-12 seconds ▶024

Sarkecards.com   edit

 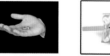
▶073
for your loved one   congrats you're not pregnant!

Improbable Sex Practice Of The Day

phobophilia \ fo-bo-fill-ee-yah \ *noun*
Sexual attraction to someone who hates homosexuals.

Found On Bahoogle Site-Seeing

And today's mystery is... Literally caught in the act. Spotted on satellite, this snaking queue of men line up outside a stadium in LA for what? Can you guess? ▶048

TranslationFish

Text to translate:

select language
- Tokyo Ritz Pillow Talk
- Marketing Speak
- Morse (Code)
- Morse (Inspector)
- Lewis (Not as good is he?)
- Ancient Geek
- That Buzz Click language some Amazon tribes speak (I saw it on a program)
- White Guy Attempting Quasimoto Impersonation near water ooler

Translate

End Of The World Countdown

10:27:43:16
YEARS   DAYS   MINUTES   SECONDS

Thank Crap I Don't Live There Daily

Half House, Falluja Contemporary demi-maisonette in sunny locale. Needs some walls. more ▶048

On This Day In History   edit

1993 Air Force Lt Colonel Helen Kellah became the first and last blind woman to pilot the space shuttler Pandemonium
more on the bolloxpedia timeline ▶066

Bahoogle Crap News   edit

Peace Virus Killions Millions ▶019

A Picture Of Some Dead Baby Swans ▶019

Hatstand

Just the word **hatstand** every day.

Like your customised homepage? Hey - you can even customise the bottom bit

owned Homepage Bahoogle by .com is Inc Bahoogle

Bahoogle
Good News

Web   Images   Group   Directory   **GoodNews**   Advanced Search

Search and browse 9,999 news sources updated continuously.

> Top Stories
Brotherhood
Of Man
Dreams
Waterfalls
Holding hands
Fireworks
Kittens

☐ News Alerts

Text Version

Top Stories

Auto-generated **25 Dec at 17:09 GMT**

World Peace sparks outpourings of joy
BBC - **1 hour ago**
Almost all of the human race were united today in a vast expression of joy in response to the newfound world peace.
In pictures: it's all smiles NCN
Hand in hand: old enemies embrace New York Yeah
World Peace - how will it affect the school run? PreserverUnlimited
Only nice people wearing flowing robes to rule the world The Lovelygraph

Bush experiences Happy Mondays
New York New York - **3 hours ago**
"He was jumping around, blowing a whistle, and kept asking me if I had any chewing gum," says Alison, 19, who danced with the President and his team of advisors at an unnamed club until 4am. "Rumsfeld gave me a kick-ass back rub."
Rice 'a bit tired' the next day but otherwise okay, say doctors NCN
Cheney smiles Christianity And Science Maintainer
XYZ Online - AllAfricanSmileyNews - CBCBNNBCBC - and 127 related

Economists retire
BCBCB - and 23 related »

Marijuana to be legalised worldwide
World Today Now (subscription) - and 19 related »

Arms industry to make vases, picnic tables
T'Scotsperson - and 178 related »

George Lucas to rewrite and re-film all three Star Wars prequels
HollywoodOutsider - and 93 related »

A lovely picture of some baby swans
Mancunian Evening News - and 21 related »

In the News

Love	Crystals
Fluffiness	Flowers
Beautiful sunsets	Lop-eared rabbits

World »

Peace Reigns in Iraq
Rheumters - **3 hours ago**
BAGHDAD, Peace has been declared in the country after both sides realised that violence never really solves anything and kissing is better.
Oil funds to be "given to the poor" The Scot
No one dies Sydney Afternoon Blarney
The Australian KnowItAll - Rheumteurs Alerts - and 127 related

Golden Age back
The Scot - **3 hours ago**
People leave their doors unlocked. Kids play on the streets. Community spirit back. Crime rate down. Drugs non-existent. Hovis Van drives slowly down cobblestone streets.
Faint sounds of a brass band heard from over t'hill Financial Snooze
Adults allowed to appreciate and play with children Gawp!
AllNewsRightNowTodayHere! - and 1 related

U.K. »

Refugees "more than welcome"
PreserverLimited - **3 hours ago**
LONDON - The UK Government today announced that street parties and country-wide festivities are to be laid on to welcome these brave people and ease their suffering.
Daily Mail, National Inquirer to shut: "hate & fear not selling" TVEye
Queen to put up 40 Armenian families in spare rooms Thisisn'tLondon
BCBC News - Xee La La - Exchellente News Italia - and 127 related

Rivers, lakes of wine and beer
Alcohol News - **3 hours ago**
An ambitious project to build three lakes, each the size of Coniston Water, and fill them with red wine, stout and lager, has begun in northern France.
Black Forest to be made of chocolate by 2030 CBCBC News
All roads turned into flower gardens Top Times Online
"No plans to reinstate motorways" WhiteVan Monthly
Washington Leveller - The Country Bore - and 115 related

Business »

Capitalists realise: "What's the point?"
Rheumters - **3 hours ago**
LONDON The Global Capitalist System fades into memory as people all over the world realise it was all a big horrible scam anyway.
Money not needed anymore Miami Cheese
Joy Index up 500 points NE.WS
The International Important NewsPaper - CNCBC - and 12227 related

All music to be free
Rheumters - **3 hours ago**
Record companies are to give away their music. Artists will give free concerts. iPODs to be given to every child at birth.
Critics resign: CD's "a matter of personal taste" CNC
Bittorrent, Emule to be built into next version of Windows Gosh
Anovabook News - Endoscopic News - and 0 related

Sci/Tech »

Environment Pristine
Rheumters - **3 hours ago**
All signs of environmental damage disappear overnight as several new inventions put everything back the way it should be.
Extinct species "coming back to life" Eco Celebrity
Hunger, disease and suffering disappear The Lance
Cancer, AIDS, vCJD all cured Scientific African
The Sundial - New Age Scientist - and 11 related

Scientists pack up: "Everything explained"
PreserverLimited - **3 hours ago**
Scientists all round the world today went home for a nice cup of tea after a revolutionary breakthrough explained everything.
The new unified theory (NUT) unites science and religion, explains genetics, the origin of the universe, quantum phenomena, and provides the first instant cure for a hangover in human history.
Scientists: "It's very simple actually, very embarrassing" New Age Scientist
Wikipedia becomes self-aware Bolloxpedia News
PC Spod - Spodwire - and 9739230 related

More top stories »

We are not alone
CBCBC - **3 hours ago**
Representatives from other planets in the galaxy were in contact with world leaders today to discuss admission in a peaceful galactic federation of planets.
Warp drive by early next year NCC
Transporters by "2050" Today Today
RussiaHappy.com - The Oz - and 1701 related

Entertainment »

Radiohead to record "happy songs"
PoutyMuse - **3 hours ago**
Critically -acclaimed rock miserablists Radiohead are to release an album of covers of happy songs from the Eighties. including "Happy Talk", "The Birdie Song", and a duet with Cliff Richard on a startling re-interpretation of his 1988 Christmas smash "Mistletoe & Wine"
The Smiths to reform MME

The selection and placement of stories on this page were determined by a beautiful young person with a wonderful heart
© Bahoogle.com - Bahoogle.com home

 **Preferences**

Save your preferences when finished

Global Preferences (changes apply to all Bahoogle services)

SafeSearch Filtering

Bahoogle's SafeSearch blocks web pages containing explicit sexual content from appearing in results. (Why?) (No, really, why?) (I mean what else are people searching for?)
- ◯ Use strict filtering (Disallow both pictures of breasts and any mention of breasts)
- ◯ Use moderate filtering (allow mention of certain breasts i.e. chicken)
- ◯ Do not filter my search results (i.e. bring on the Chest Frenzy)

Find results

with all of the	breasts	⌄
with at least one	breast	⌄
without any	penises	⌄

Return breasts

of the type	pendulous	⌄
attached to	sexy ladies	⌄
without any	bras	⌄
that are	best	⌄

Search Language

◯ Search for grotty images in any language (Recommended).

◯ Search only for grot in these languages (s)

- ▭ Czech
- ▭ Japanese
- ▭ Dutch
- ▭ Polish
- ▭ Estonian
- ▭ Russian
- ▭ French
- ▭ Swedish

Number of Results

Bahoogle's default (10 results) provides the fastest results
Display [50 ⌄] breasts per page

Booblean query

AND: Find documents containing all of the specified words or phrases. Breasts AND Butter finds pictures with both breasts and butter.

OR: Finds documents containing at least one of the specified words or phrases. Breasts OR Butter finds pictures containing either breasts or butter, so you might just get pictures of butter, and you don't really want that do you?

NOT: Excludes documents containing the specified word or phrase. Breasts NOT breasts finds pictures with nothing in them whatsoever. NOT must be used with another operator, like AND or OR or OR or... sorry lost it there for a second.

Save your preferences when finished and **return to searching for breasts**

(Note: Setting preferences will not work if you have disabled cookies in your browser.)

NEW! from our Labs **The Bahoogle Ruler** measure things on screen and that

| 0 | 100 | 200 | 300 | 400 | 500 | 600 | 700 | 800 | 900 | 1000 | 1100 | 1200 | 1300 | 1400 | 1500 |

Minimum configuration required: 1500Mhz CPU, 4.5Gb RAM, 40g hard disk, and a vast, expensive graphics card

Search and browse 4,500 news sources updated continuously.

>Top Stories
End Of World
UN.K.
Bollocks
Deep Sci/Tech
WaterSport
Schmentertainment
Poor Health

     News Alerts

     Text Version

Top Stories

Auto-generated **1st Jan at 17:09 GMT**

Peace Kills Millions
Preserver Unlimited - **1 hour ago**
World Peace and good will to all men foundered today as a mystery infection ran rampage across most of the world. The so-called 'Peace Virus', apparently spread by the hand-holding, kissing and gambolling rampant among happy people freed from the shackles of capitalism and power hungry madmen, has raged unchecked since World Peace was declared last Sunday. The death toll, already millions, continues to rise.
All frowns: who can we blame NCN
Peace Virus - how will it affect my organic box delivery? Preserver
Frightening Headlines Online – AllWorld.com - **and 600 related »**

BCBCB News

Bush in bed with 'mother of all comedowns'
New York New York - **12 hours ago**
The world was on the brink of full scale thermonuclear war as a reportedly 'bleak' American President refused to get out of bed and demanded his suitcase of nuclear launch codes. Additional reports from inside the Presidental camp indicated he was still also trying to get rid of 3 or 4 strangers whom he had invited back to party at his house.
The Morning After: Rice nixes her 'MDMA 4 ALL' Middle East peace initiative CNC
Cheney stops smiling again Buddhist Callipso Monitor
Frightening Headlines Online – AllWorld.com - **and 600 related »**

BCBCB News

Sharp rise in street crime: hooded unemployed economists blamed
Rheumters - **and 23 related »**

Marijuana legalisation: world chocolate milk shortage continues
Top Times Online (subscription) - and 19 related »

Indonesian police use picnic tables to quell riots
The Scot - and 178 related »

Rewritten Star Wars prequels to mostly detail the life and times of Jar Jar Binks
Hollywood Outsider - and 93 related »

A picture of some dead baby swans
Mancunian Evening News - and 21 related »

In the News

Rancour	Shattered glass
Matted Fur	Crushed flowers
Polluted skies	Myxomatosis

World »

Fools Golden Age?
The Scottish Paper - **3 hours ago**
Crime has sky-rocketed worldwide in the wake of people keeping their doors unlocked. Child abduction. Many blamed boredom. "Since world peace was declared we've had nothing to do," said one youth who refused to give his name.
Hovis Van involved in pile-up. Many killed. BCBCB News
Explosion at Kashmir's Happy Land theme park kills 90 Chonky's Chronicle
Pope: "If we pray it should be okay." Christianity On Fire! Daily
NowWales - **and 12 related »**

X
Washington

Aliens unmasked
Rheumters - **3 hours ago**
The peaceful space aliens purporting to come in peace from the constellation Rigel were unmasked today as human-eating space lizards on a mission to harvest food for their dying population back home.
Warp drives damage ozone layer NCD
Steve Segal turned to phlegm in prototype transporter accident XYZ News
WOWBusinessConsulting -- Russia Nice News - The Communist - **and 127 related »**

X
BBC News

U.K. »

Queen's Armenians "in the doghouse"
Preserver - **55 minutes ago**
LONDON - Attempts to integrate 40 Armenian families into the royal household have proven difficult, admitted a Buckingham Palace spokesperson. "There were some disputes over who had used the Queen's milk and over the loudness of the gyamancha music."
Leaked washing up chores list 'tampered with' EUUUU.COM
Armenian: "My Corgi Rage" The Sundial
Xinahuhuhuhhua - Channel News Asian Teens - **and 14 related »**

X
News News

Tragedy at Beer Lake
The Time Is Then (UK) - **4 hours ago**
Three teenagers drowned and one was seriously poisoned today after a boating trip on the newly formed Beer Lake ended in tragedy. "It appears the youngsters decided to go for a swim," said a local lifeguard spokesperson, "and, well, you can guess what happened."
Lake Chardonnay closed pending healthy and safety inspection Times A Changing Online
Chocolate Black Forest devoured by roaming stoners BCBCB
Belfast Shouty - Sydney Morning Dollop - **and 28 related »**

X
GAH!

Entertainment »

Radiohead happy album tanks
PreserverUnlimited - **11 hours ago**
Radiohead were unavailable for comment today as news came in that Radiohead's latest LP "Smiley Smiley Chin Hurts" had only sold 40 copies. A record company spokesperson blamed the breakdown of capitalism and worldwide resignation of critics for the plummeting sales.
"Worse than Amnesiac " Rheumters
"The Smiths to reform" NMAH
Telegraph.po.le - ZIP News -**and 93 related »**

Rheumters

Sci/Tech »

Scientists back in: "Everything not explained"
BCBCB News - **0.3 femtoseconds ago**
Scientists all round the world today put down their cups of tea and tutted after flaws were discovered in the new unified theory (NUT). "The hangover cure, in particularly, is deeply flawed," said one scientist. "New tests reveal that it causes cancer and an especially nasty rash on the backs of the knees."
Dwarkins: "String theory complete bobbins but better than this muck " NewAge Scientist
Self-aware Wikipedia launches pre-emptive nuclear strike on humanity Scientific Creationist
PC Spod - Mac Smug Daily News - **and 99 related »**

BBC News

Bahoogle Home ◀015 - All About Bahoogle - About Bahoogle News

404 The page cannot be found

The page you are looking for might have been removed. Perhaps you
tore it out because you were laughing so much? You know, tears in your
eyes. Your lumpen cloddish fists mauling the page with blind, uncontrollable
hilarity? Well, you might have done.

Please try one of the following:

- Close the book, wait for five seconds then reopen it again.
- Open the contents page 008 and then look for links
  to the information you want.
- Turn ⇦ Back to the previous page and then PageTurn forward
  to this page once more.

PTTP 404 - Page not found
The Internet Now In Handy Book Form!

Your account   Current order   Saved Orders   Order Status   Help

Schmapple Store

Search 🔍

 Try our new Search

Special Offers

Unleash the creative

Ever dreamt of be a musician? Of course you have. Now you can live out that dream in your den with DreamOnPro ▶047
Try it today

In our forums

"My McC's better than" yours."

"No, it bloody isn't."

"Well, I've got three McC's!"

"Butt out, fanboy."

"Steve is God! "

"Mine's never crashed"

"Mine did once. I cried"

All products available in these shades

Incredible White
Fantabulous White
Virginal White
Snow White
Cyphocilus White
Black

Introducing. . .

sign off in style

suicide has never been this slick or easy ▶046

all change

nervous using your Schmapple product in public? We've got the solution! ▶022

Why settle for less?

Override all iZods within a given radius with your choice of music

iRule
For McC, not PC

Now 100 metre range for £299 and 200 metres for £399 INC VAT

Steve Jobs Altar

AltarPro now shipping

iBruprofen

sleek lightweight painkillers

iMams know best

Schmapple priests for all occasions

---

iZod store ▶022

Accessories	Utility Belt	incomprehensible bits	Just the headphones
iZod maxi ▶022	just like Batman's	just buy them, okay?	get mugged too

---

iTug

firewire masturbation machine with three nozzles

Void in style

sleek polycarbonate toilet with silent flush

The sky's the limit

Project your desktop on the heavens 800 miles (798 viewable)

The Schmapple Mysteron

Inexplicable brushed-titanium box with a single, tiny green flashing light. Does nothing but looks great. Perfect talking piece for the living room or to put in the corner of an architect's reception area.

Rub it in with iSmug

10 high definition screensavers made by top Hollywood directors honouring Schmapple's superior technology. Includes: Spike Jonze's 'Click Wheel', Darren Aronofsky on the Expose function and Michel Gondry: 'The Eternal Lightness Of My 15" McCBook (With Superdrive)'

iMug

Polished-steel rod that delivers 12,000 volts of electric death to anyone who even brushes your iZod. Available in a range of pleasing pastel colours. Based on technology developed by the Malaysian Government.

McCPhone

The wait is over! The Schmapple handset is finally here. It's a movie player, an iZod, a portable games machine, a USB hard-drive, a camera. Wait, did we miss something out?

Welcome,

Sign in or create your own personal account
Sign up for 1-Click

Best sellers

- iZod femto ▶022
- iZod mondo ▶022
  iZod maxi ▶022
* iZod pillow case and quilt cover
* iZod blowup
* mattress and pillow
* iZod T-shirt
  iZod pants
* iZod-shaped wedding cake
  iZod lilo
. iZod chewing gum
. iZod muscle vest
. iZod panties
  iZod cushions
- iZod punchbag
- iZod on toast

New To The Store

cables
beautiful cables
such beautiful cables

Schmapple Therapy

Instant onsite counselling when your McC is stolen

YogaMcC

It's a mat
It's a McC!

In Your Dreams

Download and watch from the Schmapple store with AstralZod

iBok

Alright alright well you try to come up with 50 i-jokes

The new size iZods

We've been improving our technology and listening to our customers. You wanted bigger iZods, so we're giving you bigger iZods. We're also introducing our smallest iZod yet – a mere twelve microns across!

iZod maxi

Completely, ludicrously, heavy. but just about portable.
From $68,000

iZod mondo

Call the police!
1, 2 and 4 Brontobytes
From $149,000

iZod femto

Actual size as shown
From $149
Insurance: $9999

Schmapple Changing Rooms

Worry about changing tracks or untangling your headphones in public? Worry no longer as Apple Changing Rooms appear on every major public transport network in the world. They're safe air-conditioned bubbles to keep you and your Apple product out of reach of prying eyes and jealous, fat, greasy poor people's fingers.

How do wear yours?

In the 21st century the way your iZod hangs says a more about you than your lifestyle, your clothes or your sexual preference. Perhaps. The trouser pocket and 'inside the bag' are out. *So* 20th century. These new hanging styles are in.

the standard

Easy to access but prone to fall out especially when leaning over to give tech advice to the attractive new intern.

twin shooter

30G on the left, 60G on the right. Never know when you might need the storage. Very popular at McCWorld.

drug deal

Slippage into the bum cleft is a real peril, but this rear position is *rigueur* with fashionistas and budding Jack Bauers.

LAPD

Walking can be difficult. Skipped tracks are very common. Throttling by headphone cables too. But looks cool, so that's okay.

the buscadero

Folding in the classic Latino look with modern technology, the ammo belt look is for the rich discerning show off. Chewing match optional.

tune your life

iLifeCoach

Transform your iPod into a personal life coach and reap the results instantly! A wireless sensor, receiver and a shouty voice in your ear can work miracles for achieving your goals in life. Believe us. We'd have never got this bloody book done without it.

tune

orientate

live

compare

yeah!

tune Strap the wireless sensor to your heart and then plug the receiver to the your iPod.

orientate Select the goal category you want to work on, or just choose 'Random' if your life is a mess.

live Live your life while your heart sensor tracks your needs. Real time speech gives you constant feedback

voices available: Female computer voice from Alien R. Lee Emery, Simon Cowell.

compare Upload your successes online. Get instant feedback and see how much better others are doing.

yeah! America. Sweet America. Land of the free and true. America, Sweet America, dah dee dah doo..

Our Beautiful Wedding
Darren & Sara

Welcome to the official website of the marriage of Darren Edward Marshall, and Sara Lorraine Osman. We got married on the 23rd January 1999, which is when our anniversary now is. This was the happiest day of both our lives, and we invite you to re-live the sheer joy we felt on that special day through the medium of HTML. We hope that through this webpage you will feel some of the sheer joy we felt on that wonderful day. Our life together as husband and wife has begun.

OUR STORY
After meeting each other at a medieval battle re-enactment where I took Sara prisoner but waived my right to rape her, we quickly found we had a lot in common: when my grandfather had a stroke in Luton shopping centre in 1992, Sara's mother had been there by chance and stood around helplessly until the paramedics arrived. Spooky!

stag and hen parties
I was worried that my friend Dave would arrange a stag night that I would find embarrassing, as I'm a quiet man who enjoys the simple things in life. I needn't have worried – he booked us tickets to a midget stripping and wrestling show in a secluded barn just off the A23. It was brilliant. Thanks, Dave!.

the wedding!!!!
The theme of our wedding was Fire And Ice. I was fire, Sara was ice, as was her mum, Dave the best man was fire, the vicar was ice, my mum was fire and so on. There were ice arches at the entrance to the church, the altar was made of ice, there were buckets of ice everywhere, and my trousers were ON FIRE!

honeymoon
We had an amazing honeymoon, an 11-month stay in the Horton House Bed & Breakfast in Stoke Poges, which is rated 14th on the "Most Romantic Bed & Breakfast In Stoke Poges" website, and 6th in the "Best Place To Have Hesitant Indoor First-Time Sex In And Around Stoke Poges" information booklet. They were right! I would say it's at least the 14th and 6th best respectively. [Read more...]

THE PROPOSAL
I took Sara to a secret place that we have which we call "Our Secret Place", and I asked her to marry me. She said "Oh yes, Darren, yes, and in Our Secret Place, too, yes, secret, yes," and we literally jumped into each others arms, hovering above the ground for several seconds in sheer joy.

the preparation
You wouldn't believe how much time we've spent on getting the cake, the dresses and the flowers exactly the way Sara wanted! Fortunately we've taken photos of everything, and I mean everything, from several different angles, using various settings on the camera, just to make absolutely sure the cake, dresses and flowers are never forgotten, by anyone.

our hymn
We are getting married
In this big church
It is big and old, its true
A biggy oldy church
Churchy, churchy, wedding-ding
Ding-a-ding-a-wedding ring
Ring! Ring! Church wed
Then weddy-beddy-wedding bed

PROTECT YOUR CHILDREN
FROM THE KNOWLEDGE THAT YOU DO DRUGS

- Knowing your limits
- Phoning your dealer quietly
- Keeping tabs in a locked box
- How to spot drugs
- What to do if you run out
- Selling to other parents
- Guides, books & glowsticks

"My son caught me blowing meth up my wife's ass..."
Click for pics ▶118

5 WAYS TO HIDE YOUR HABIT FROM YOUR KIDS

Our Mission

Your child's innocence is paramount
We partner with families to inspire more parents and family members to conceal their drug use - medicinal, recreational and occasional party - from their kids. That way we can protect children from the knowing the truth. This, we believe, will help them to make a less informed, clumsier, more impulsive decision to experiment with drugs when they're good and ready. At college, say. Or at the bottom of the garden at a party. Yeah somewhere like that.

Use These Filter-Less Tips

1 Get some dull churchy friends for the day. Save cool friends for night time.

2 Wear a suit at all times.

3 Use hideously outdated euphemisms for drugs: "jazz cigarettes" "disco biscuits" etc.

4 De-hippy your house. Lose the afghan hound, the Tolkien books and anything to do with Buddhism.

5 Get some Carpenters tracks. Play them.

URGENT: New Street Drugs Advisory

Look out for these new street drugs so, er if you find them on your child, you can quickly recognise them and put them 'beyond use'.

Talk To Your Kids In The Right Way

At the core of good parenting is good communication and honesty. So when pushed, remember the bottom line: "Just Say 'No'".

"Normal E-Tea" Gives a focused, centered feeling. Often taken with lots of sugar to mask the bitter taste. **Side effects**: Biscuit cravings. **Duration**: 8-12 years.

"Edge-E" Feelings of being not quite high nor not quite normal. "Like queuing for a toilet at a festival while watching 24". **Side effects**: Hopping, wringing hands. **Duration**: 8-12 hours.

"Schadenfreude" An appetite-for-revenge suppressant gives a delicious full body high and a clenched perma-smile. **Side effects**: Glinty eyes. **Duration**: 8-12 weeks.

"Time Travel" Experimental US Army psychotropic with out-of-body effects. **Side effects**: Banal adventures in other peoples' bodies. **Duration**: 8-12 seasons.

"Creamy Dinner" Fluffy 'full' feeling. Users also suffer severe 'couchlock' and must be sat down with a cigar and slippers. **Side effects**: Constipation. **Duration**: 8-12 weekends.

"Confidex" Diverted anti-anxiety medicine extracted from Meerkat pineal gland. Triggers intense career progression. **Side effects**: Psychosis, depression. **Lasts**: 8-12 mins.

sample conversation 01 - "the white lie"
"Dad, have you taken drugs?"
"Well I did grow up in the 90s!"
"So you did take some?"
"Well I was offered dear, of course, but I always said [cough, cough]"
"Always said what?"
"I answered you, love petal."
"No. I didn't hear. You were coughing. Always said what?"
[cross your fingers behind your back. This is a Vatican-approved way of 'white lying']
"No. I always said 'no'".
"Really?"
"Yes."

conversation 02 - "the game"
"Mummy, why is Uncle Tim dancing on the table?"
"He's just very happy dear. As am I!"
"What are those things on your chest?"
"What? Oh these? Oh they're tassles, dear. It's for a game we're playing."

conversation 03 - "the art"
"Did any of your friends take drugs daddy?"
"Yes. Yes they did."
"What happened to them?"
"They all ended up in the Arts."
"Is that like being ill?"
"It's a kind of illness, yes."

Read more about new drugs

Read more sample conversations ◀105

poormatch.com

The worst dating site in the world

welcome loveseekers

Looking for love online? You won't find it here. Fancy being put through the emotional wringer and experiencing a unique cocktail of hope and despair? You've come to the right place!

Over one million people have had lukewarm romantic encounters since joining Poormatch.com. Millions more spend desultory evenings looking at poorly taken JPEGs, projecting their fantasies onto other helpless, desperate people, often drunkenly. Through gritted teeth.

Why not join today?

Quick Search

I am a: **woman**

Seeking: **wretched throwaway sex**

located within **20** miles of **city/postco**

Online ☐   MingFilter ☑   **Search now**

Success Stories

"We met online and literally within seconds we were regetting exchanging mobile phone numbers and email addresses. Thank you Poormatch!"
Belinda1973

"I've met some really freaky people through PoorMatch and picked up a couple of stalkers along the way! Thanks so much for your service and for your support."
Hilary

"Following many amusing and threatening email exchanges Gary finally tracked me down to my home address. After a brief siege and some arson he had me."
Belinda1973

"FGyahhhaggg. Where are all the men? I've been on this site. Nothing. Not even a wink."
CEO ▶028

New Profiles

 YeahMan I'm a typical Saggiterian. I can't spell. I bump into joists. I love bums and am easily led by cheerless new-age flim flam. Ole!

 Colonic I do yoga. I mediate 10 hours a day. I run, skip and jump. I eat 60 portions of fruit and veg a day, and floss after every meal and every bowel movement and every date. That's a promise sister.

 LittleDreamerBoy Hey and thanks for tuning in! I've got my head in the clouds, feet on the ground, world at my feet, and cock in my hand!

Schizoid I'm told, by myself, that I'm a good person to know and we think that's a pretty fair assessment. But then I would because we wrote it.

 CosyNites I'm an film-junkie alcoholic with scoliosis of the spine so I like nothing better than curling up on the sofa with a bottle of red wine and a DVD.

 MountainMan I can build fire, strip and cook bush meat, swim four lengths under water, climb a mountain backwards. Due to work I can't actually emotionally commit to anyone.

 TrashyManky I like trashy nights out and dirty nights in. Gigs and parties. Anything to keep me from taking responsibility for my life. (I'm 39)

 Minx I love friends, candy, dancing and butterflies!!! Holding hands, shooting stars, bubble baths, make up, girly mags, cloud shapes, and scat play.

How It Works

1 Lurk on the site for weeks

Alternate between doe-eyed optimism and lonely self-loathing, until the exhortations of your bored friends and family force you to take the plunge.

2 Take 1000s of photos
Too fat. Too thin. Too many spots. You're glad you shelled out for Photoshop. Plump for the least awful one, taken on holiday in Thailand 16 years ago.

5 On the hamster wheel

Discover the modern thrill of rejection, paranoia and obsession as you desperately try to maintain bonds with elusive fancy people by sending ever more self-conscious emails and texts over a period of weeks and months.

Poormatch.com makes finding love as painful as possible. Here's how it works.

3 Upload your profile and get it on!

Check every six minutes for hits, winks and emails. Receive none. Feel an enormous sense of emptiness, the kind only three large packets of Mango Chilli Kettle Chips can fill.

4 Go on your first date

Meet at a poorly chosen venue. Get helplessly drunk due to nerves. Have wretched throwaway sex just to feel alive. Forget to use a condom.

poormatch.com

The worst dating site in the world

Our Sister Sites

doggr ™ Share car parks and grotty couples online

BreakingDirect.com
painlessly chuck your partner with one click

NO PHOTO lotto

MAGICK DATING ▶064
MIDDLE WORLD'S PREMIERE PERSONALS SERVICE

mantrap
GOLD DIGGERS
CHILDLESS BUNNY BOILERS
SEDUCTRICES
MURDERESSES

CARBON DATING
save the world and your love life ▶

Baby Baby Baby NOWNOWNOW

ZERO GRAVITY DATING
on a Russian cargo plane in the troposphere anything can happen...

WORLDS SHITTEST MEN

Sponsored Links

▸ Witty But Hideous
▸ You'll Do
▸ Desperate Lonely People Yearning For Connection Through Technology
▸ The Best Dating Site In The World (U.S. only)
▸ Stalk Me - I Likee
▸ This Is All A Bit Like The Circuit In Logan's Run Isn't It?

Edit Your Profile

My Portrait

Stick your photo here

My Portrait

And another photo here (from a slightly different angle)

My Profile

Name

Tagline

About You

About who you're looking for

Send your finished profile to http://www.theinternetnowinhandybookform.com

Currently Online

« previous   page 1 of 5,039,099,153   next »

dangerman
currently: bulk emailing 9000 girls
▶027

masterfulcock69
currently: masturbating into a sports sock while thinking of old girlfriends

suffocator
currently: getting an 18 year old's number
▶027

billygoatsgruff
currently: coming up dry

stalker9000
currently: substantially older than this picture

TooHottForThisSite
currently: dismissing people for the tiniest flaw

mollybloom
currently: sighing
▶028

pricktease
currently: waiting 4 u
▶084

vodkafairy
currently: drunk
▶084

sophia from arabia
currently: on fire!

got an itch? ➤ bit of a headache? ➤ feeling HOT? ➤ **probably SYPHILLIS**

National **H**ypochondriacs **S**ervice
here to help ▶054

Poormatch Profile

Dangerman
Stand in awe of my phenomenal power

Active within 1 minute
32-year-old man seeking women 18-19

About Me

I live on the edge. I put myself in dangerous situations. I thrive on danger. I give wedgies to fear and Chinese Burns to Death. At weekends I work with highly combustible materials, and then, for relaxation, I drag heavy goods vehicles through Richmond Park using only my teeth. I also lift weights with my penis. Not proud about that but I do it. I do stand proudly on the banks of rivers in a tight wetsuit, however, looking for helpless women bobbing about in distress, while preparing to mount a thrilling rescue attempt. I flex my muscles, and when I've flexed them once, I flex them again. Watch. See? Yeah.

About who I'm looking for

Whoever. Whenever.

More about me

Interests:	Explosions, teetering on a precipice
Job	Librarian
Eyes:	Eagle
Foreplay:	a gruelling 12-hour marathon
Perfect Date:	human cannonball lessons (intermediate), rock climbing (with no rope and no rock)
Celebrity I most resemble:	Hasel DavidHoff (before BeachWatch)
Favourite possessions:	My washboard stomach, my washboard

Poormatch Profile

Suffocator
That got your attention, didn't it?

Active all the time
30-year-old man seeking any woman as long as she'll love him

About Me

I'll cook you Eggs Benedict every morning. I'll kiss your fingertips for hours on end. When you are out or just out of my sight, I'll believe that you're going to die, and demand that you text me every fifteen minutes just so I know your precious heart is still beating. Our relationships will be all about presents, love, hand holding and affection in public. And I'll always ask your permission before I go out with any of my friends or talk to another woman.

About who I'm looking for

Soft, cuddly, indoorsy goddess whom I can fuse with. I'm 110% committed to my partners and like to spend loads of time together. There's no such thing as 'me time' if you love someone, right?

More about me

Interests:	you and only you
Job:	loving
Hobbies:	coming up with cutsie names for my loved such as 'schnooky lips' and 'puppy queen'
Perfect Date:	staring into each other's eyes, lengthy bout of hand holding, then washing your feet for two hours
Outlook:	Lovely
On my bookshelf:	A picture of you in a gold frame with some of those flowers that open when you clap

Poormatch Profile

WackyDude
stupid, unfunny, brutish, balding layabout

Active within 24 hours
36-year-old man seeking any woman who can take continuous, unabating irony and japery all day and all night

About Me

Only joking! I'm actually handsome, brainy and creative and FUNNY! So why are you single? I hear you cry! Well, I'm a bit closed and easily hurt so the only way I can tolerate being on this site is by hiding behind my wacky sense of humour. So here goes. What am I like? Well picture Hitler and then picture the Dalai Lama, I'm some where in between. Random fact: I get a curious surge when I pull over for ambulances in heavy traffic. Don't ask me why. And here's what my friends say about me: "He's a cock. Don't date him." Oh cheers you f**ks! Joking!

About who I'm looking for

Own teeth, own hair, own lips - that's a good start! You can catch a frisbee. Good at thumb-war. If you've got those slightly webbed sort of toes, don't respond. Joking! You must like the word 'elbow'. Joking! Is this thing still on???! Joking!

More about me

Interests:	Knitting
Books:	Self-help!
Eyes:	Two.
Perfect Date:	ripe but not too squishy!
Outlook:	Nah, I'm a Eudora man.
Retirement plans :	Dying, alone, of a terrible disease. Joking!

Poormatch Profile

Widower
I can't believe she's gone

Active within 24 hours
35-year-old man seeking release from grief sodden existence

About Me

My wife Julie died last week, but I feel that I'm finally ready to have a bit of fun dating other women. I enjoy working with clay, sculpting replicas of my late wife's head in particular. Day after day I spend sculpting, carefully using a scalpel to perfectly capture the upturned tilt of her nose.

About who I'm looking for

Ideally, someone who looks like my late wife – blonde, with beautiful, cascading golden hair that tumbles around your creamy shoulders as you throw back your head.... laughing gaily as the sun shines into your sparkling eyes. Oh, Julie....Yes Julie.... someone like Julie.

More about me

Interests:	Mourning, wailing, hoping
Eyes:	Damp
Work:	On compassionate leave
Perfect Date:	A long drive through the country to my late wife's tomb
Outlook:	Gloomy with scattered showers
Things I couldn't live without:	Julie

THE 14th ANNUAL WORLD SPEED DATING GAMES
Events include: Discus (Hobbies), Toe Curling, The 5000m Chuck

poormatch.com

▼ MY POORMATCH   SEARCH   MY MESSAGES   MY ACCOUNT   HELP   PLEASE

The worst dating site in the world

more profiles ▶085

CELEBRITIES IN TREES

Which German tennis ace? Which famous tv comedy duo? Which renown spiritual leader?

It's the new celebrity craze, it is.

Poormatch Profile

DreamCatcher
Don't be a Taurean in a china shop

Active within 24 lunar cycles.
32-year-old woman seeking Scorpios and Librans ONLY

About Me

I'm a Taurus....I am of a New Age..Don't you feel it!? I share love with all that need it...Do you need it?. I LOVE to spend time with beautiful people who express themselves through the medium of beauty....Ah....so much love in the world....I love to create items that connect to the magic within like crystals, dreamcatchers, fairy wings, fairy outfits. While meditating, I receive often messages from the stone and crystal people....Words that resonate with me: Spirituality. Healing. Totems. Feng Shui. Goji Berries. I pick up nuggets of meaning from any Eastern philosophies that waft through my cerebral vortex and I adopt them as my own. I call my new religion "Su". Will you be "Su" too?

About who I'm looking for

Plumbers...gas fitters..doormen.....barmen....plasterers (yum!)....Painters and decorators....window cleaners....electricians...um...forklift truck drivers. Anyone with oily hands and a pelvis like a washing machine. Oo yeah!!!!!!!!

More about me

Starsign:	Taurus of course! Silly
Height:	5"2'
Religion:	my own
Decor?	Scented candles, scented soaps, scented bin liners
Eyes:	Green
Status:	Green

Poormatch Profile

Molly Bloom
writer and recherchist

Active within 24 hours
27-year-old woman seeking artists, raconteurs, dilettantes 26-60

About Me

So I sit down to pen this profile, fingering tusks of absinthe and dried tears from my eyes. Home-made aioli and pitta bread lay disconsolately in a bowl beside my drumming fingers. This is my profile, I realise. All mine. No one else's. Still in my flannelette pyjamas, me, the dilettante dater. I bought a large chocolate cake with the words 'arrivederci' spooled across it in child-like icing handwriting. Can't you chefs learn to write proper? I quipped in the shop. They just stared at me. My day? White on black. Running my hand across the smooth onyx of my piano, running my legs across the crumpled tarmacadam of Putney village, running my fantasies across the stiff limbs of a West Indian man. All this aside, I like nothing better than lounging across my chaise longe with a bottle of Sauvignon and a unsubtitled version of the Werckmeister Harmonies.

About who I'm looking for

Still in flannelette I take a book to the Common: Saul Bellow, Jhumpa Lahiri, Joyce. Sigh. The tyranny of choice. Rising to the fridge to fetch my rosehip cordial, I snag a thread of the arm of my linen shirt and resolve to either a) sand the chair; b) get a new chair; or c) get a fucking life.

More about me

Relationships:	Never had one.
Have kids:	None. The noise-making sacks of organs.
Want kids:	Eight. Hopefully someday
Ethnicity:	White / Caucasian / Milky
Perfect Date:	A tour of Highgate Cemetry name-dropping poets, snuffling for recherche items in the troughs of Borough Market and then recourse to my boudoir to sing sea shanties and toast the recalcitrant dawn.
Smoke:	Filterless.Gitanes
Drink:	Constantly.

Poormatch Profile

Cath
Vicar's daughter

Active within 24 hours
24-year-old woman seeking charismatic masterful men 26-48

About Me

Hi, I'm Cath. Like 'Catholic', which is why my father named me that. He's a vicar, you know. Of course you know, it's in the tagline. Anyway, that means I'm a 'nice girl', though I'm not a full on member of the GOD SQUAD(tm). Look I put 'Agnostic' in my religious preferences (so naughty!!!) Sorry dad.
Anyway, I work in a worthy occupation helping poor uneducated people who didn't go to as good a school as me. Some of them don't even have A levels, LET ALONE GOD! I am a lot of fun but I have a bit of a hangup about my small breasts, but will never admit it.
p.s quite a few people recently have asked about my sexuality, and I'd like to make it clear that I'm not a lesbian. There was that time in the sixth form dorm when I accidentally brushed Emilia Clayton's breast whilst reaching for my night braces, but that's absolutely it??!?
I like nothing better than curling up on the sofa with a quart of purloined communion wine and a DVD.

About who I'm looking for

A God.

More about me

Relationships:	Yes please!
Have kids:	None
Want kids:	Loads and loads.
Perfect date:	night at a BDSM / Karaoke club

Poormatch Profile

CEO
come on then if you're hard enough

Active within 24 hours
36-year-old woman seeking a decent bloody man! 26-48

About Me

Glamorous, intelligent, creative, successful with a big heart and lot of affection to give and give and give. Likes film, rocks and stimulant drugs, yoga, rock-climbing, mountaineering and any physical pursuits that stretch me. I'm open minded and quite liberal in my views. But no drug addicts or lefties per-lease! I'm also a good and empathic listener who tends to put myself first. Serious about career, money, my house and all the things that matter. Also couldn't live without laughs, sillyness and those Youtube clips of kittens falling off sofas.

I like nothing better than dominating the chocolate leather armchair in my large empty house with a bottle of red and a Ghostbusters DVD.

About who I'm looking for

He should enjoy serious discouse and high, sharp slaps across the face and neck.

More about me

Relationships:	Never Married
Have kids:	None
Want kids:	Yes!
Happiest when:	Being towelled down by a huge, hairy Turkish bloke
Body type:	About average
Perfect date:	meet and greet, nibbles, pre-interview chat, short battery of cognitive test, family questionnaire, drinks, sperm donation

---

Needy? Panic-stricken? Consumed by self-loathing? justByou.co.uk ▶044
because no-one else wants to be

---

note: poormatch.com cannot be held responsible for any freakazoids, jocks, weirdos, bong nancies and oiks you may meet on this site
poormatch.com is a wholly owned upholstered gimp of Bahoogle.com

028

BROWSE

Children's Books
- Aged 4-8
- Aged 9-12
- Aged 13-16
- Men aged 17-48 ▶096

Fiction
- Medieval Ones Where A Monk Is A Detective
- Ponderous Inner Thoughtscapes
- Highly Strung Over Thinky People Not Getting What They Want
- See More...

Health & Spirituality
- Health, Mind, & Body & Spirit & Love & Light & Life & You At The Centre Of It All Drumming With Your Top Off

Lifestyle, Family, & Home
- Cooking, Food, & Wine
- Arguing, Slamming Doors & Plotting Revenge
- Browsing, Downloading & Wanking
- Quiet Desperation, TV and a bottle of red

Book Accessories
- Hands
- Eyes
- An imagination

Special Formats
- Books on Toilet Paper
- Books on Special Edition Vinyl
- Large Print
- Very Large Print
- Extremely Large Print: You Know Like A Letter A Page Something Like That

My What A Huge Cook

Hot off the stove, Nigella Fellatrix's latest creation: Double Cream Down My Cleavage. Buy it today and get My Bum? On A Fridge Shelf absolutely free.
> More cream Prime Minister?

Bill Bison On The Internet

Everyone's favourite explorer crosses the final frontier ▶052

Hello. Sign in to get personalized recommendations. Sign out to get free of this eerie know-it-all database.

Best Sellers

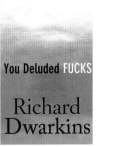

You Deluded FUCKS
Richard Dwarkins

The world's cleverest man speaks his mind.

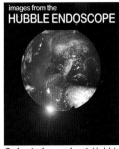

images from the HUBBLE ENDOSCOPE

Order today and get Hubble Esophagogastroduodenoscopy: A Pictoral Journey free!

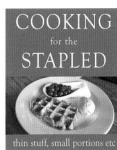

COOKING for the STAPLED

thin stuff, small portions etc

Every host's nightmare - solved

Popular subjects

THE MASSIVE UNDERSELL BIG CLASSIC
OH JUST STOP EATING CAKES & RUN A BIT
DR ROGER CANT M.D.

Dieting
- The Class A Diet
- The Buboe Diet
- The Book That's A Meal - Just Read Then Microwave

I WAS ON TV
for a bit

Celebrity Hagiography
- I Kick A Ball
- I Have Tits
- I Slept With Somebody

momentary enthusiasms
Rowing Machine

White Elephant Books
Interests to take up and jettison shortly afterwards
- Bonsai Tree
- Pond
- Juicer
- Ethnic Friends

Mash-Up Books: Women's Horror

THE DAY I LOST MY BAG

The latest literary sensations hits the streets as the world famous Mash-Up books produce another masterpiece. Best selling Woman's Horror novelist Stephanie Queen's latest title is a by-the-seat-of-your-pants page turner. "As scary as a stalker posting you his own shit every day or so" said one of our reviewers. Order today and get her previous, chilling best-seller free.

BOYS! GEEK HORROR SPECIAL OFFER
Order She Downloaded Some Toolbar today and get She Dissed Kurzweil for just $19.00!

HE ENDED IT BY TEXT
STEPHANIE QUEEN

Reference Guides

THE POWER OF NAH
A GUIDE TO SPIRITUAL PROCRASTINATION
Eckhart Dole

Don't Self-Help
- Not Getting Things Done
- The Seven Habits Of Highly Successful Heroin Addicts
- Feel The Fear: Run Away
- The Piss Artist's Way

THE ROUGHEST GUIDE TO
Sandpaper

The Roughest Guide To
- Emery Board
- Approximation
- No lube anal quickies
- Baghdad

1001 HORRIBLE WAYS YOU COULD DIE BEFORE YOU DIE

The 1001 Range
- 1001 Places To Visit Before You Die (Hodder)
- 1002 Things To See Before You Die (Penguin)
- 2002 Places To Visit Before You Die (Hodder)
- 10,001 Things To See Before You Die (Penguin)
- Infinity Places To Visit Before You Die (Hodder)
- Infinity Plus One Things To See Before You Die (Penguin)

Coffee Table

Male Circumcision
A PICTORIAL HISTORY

Be the talk of the street with these luscious best-selling full-colour books. Lovingly compiled by some of the world's greatest pornographers, they are a real talking point for the lounge or the hairdresser.

Impossible Chords

You visit someone's house. There's a guitar lying there, so you pick it up and start showing off. When you've finished, the guitar's owner takes it back and shows off about ten times better than you just did. Bastard! What you need to give this person is The Impossible Chord Book. This should undermine his confidence to the point where he gives up playing guitar, goes mad and eventually takes his own life.

Amasszone.com Top 100
Updated hourly

TELETEXT now in handy book form

1. Teletext: Now In Handy Book Form $14.99
2. Paul McKennot: I Can Make You Vomit $14.99
3. JK Rowing: The Really Big Read For The Train Ride In To Work $16.20
4. This Diary Will Change Your Diary 2008 $14.97
5. The Ark Of The Covenant Diet $14.99

> All top sellers

Top Selling PC Software
Updated hourly

Arrest Me Pro

> more great software ▶070

COCOON
FOR MEN

HOME	GARAGE	DEN	COMPUTER	BLACK BOXES	WIRES

NEW!

Phone with manual bigger than handset

£120 Order

NEW!

Framed poster of the classic science fiction film

£110 Order

SPECIAL OFFERS

Fourteen yards of Scalextric nailed to a huge lump of hardboard in your loft (includes cars from The Ducks Of Hazzard, Starsky PI and Knight Driver)

£110 Order

Enough CD shelving to fill the whole of the spare room and leave no room to put a cot in there.

£110 Order

SECRET TREKKIE BOX

A box of DVDs that, while critically acclaimed, are actually just full of robots and spaceships, including: *Terminator V: This Time I'm Back To Find Out Why You Hug*

Find out more

Welcome gadget seekers!

It's a big scary world out there: full of responsibilities, difficult situations and death. But you simply don't want to face it.

If you'd rather have kid's toys delivered direct to your door and spend your weekends playing with remote-controlled AV technology, you've come to the right place!

THIS WEEK'S BARGAINS

Sound And Vision   More

Pair of top decks for you to use 2-3 times and then leave ostentatiously in your living room so you can tell visitors that you're a DJ.

£575.99   Order

Lifestyle   More

A ridiculous two-seater car that simply screams "no room for children or shopping!"

£25,999.99 Order

Décor   More

A banana-seated Raleigh Chopper or orange 'frowning' Space Hopper to lean against the wall of your lounge or reception area in an amusingly kitsch way.

£150   Order

Sound And Vision   More

NADS Hi-Fi system with everything connected through everything else so you can watch Animaniacs in Quad Surround or record your doorbell digitally to minidisc.

£789.95   Order

Leisure   More

A StayPlation 360 with vibrating controllers and tons of games where you play a man running around shooting things, blowing things up and saving the world. Fantasy-tastic!

£239.99   Order

COCOON SPECIAL COLLECTIONS
Pocket money gifts at adult salary prices

Brrm! Brrm!
Twelve shiny die-cast cars, just a tiny bit bigger than Corgi used to make them, displayed under low-lighting on individual glass shelves.
£999.99
Order

The Low Brow Collection
A collection of movies that wouldn't tax the attention span of a 5 year old full of Sunny Delight. Includes: The Matrix, Die Hard, Face/Off.
£1007.24
Order

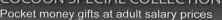

REMEMBER!
Your second childhood comes in a big exciting looking box that can be turned into a fort afterwards.

Dollies For Men

A selection of 'collectible' figurines, brought to you by the same people who sell your gran china dogs out of the back of Sunday newspaper magazines.

Scents For Men

ONE NIGHT STAND

LAN PARTY
POUR HOMME

SHE'S AWAY FOR THE WEEK END

Answer:

COCOON
FOR MEN

HOME   GARAGE   DEN   COMP...

NEW!

Take the effort, strain and tangle out of having a laugh in the park with these new wireless kites. Uses the latest hi-bandwidth 802.11x protocol. Note: may interfere with laptops and fun.

Order

NEW!

Unified Controller
At last! For the gadget head who has literally everything - a single remote universal control for all your gadgets. Weighs just 14 kilos..

£110   Order

JUMP GAPS
shoot people
Collect Coins
FIGHT A BIT

essential videogaming

TOTAL GAME LORD
▶043

Laptop Self Destruct

Is there anything more humiliating than being caught masturbating over Internet porn by your partner? No. And the only solution? Instant death via the wireless Laptop Self-Destruct.

£2999.99

Order

Technol...

Video gaming

YBox 1440 Just in from the future is the YBOX 1440. Send emails back and forth in time. Project a fantasy of your imaginings on a wall. Record your dreams. And attach the teledildonic riser to your chair to cyber with hott android chicks from the year 2929.

£299.99   Order

Gadgets   More

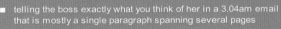

Summer Blinkers
Avoid ugly accusations and broken relationships in summer time with these easy-fit blinders. Just like a horse, these easy fit blinder minimise distracted by whatever may be in your peripheral vision: the swaying effects of gravity, for example, or the soft compress of a young breast against a tight summery top.
Made of black leather.

£69.99   Order

FEATURED PRODUCTS

The Broadband Breathylser

Works by preventing users from accessing the Internet if their blood alcohol readings are higher than 0.08 mg. Above this level, cyber-standards begin to drop considerably.

This can lead to errors of judgement including:

- telling the boss exactly what you think of her in a 3.04am email that is mostly a single paragraph spanning several pages
- printing out that sexy ICQ chat with the cute Dutch bloke then leaving it in the printer for your bf or gf to find
- cybersex with fat Americans in bad jumpers

The Broadband Breathylser offers full protection from mailing whilst mashed. Nips drunken flame wars in the bud. And no more shameful splling mistaks. Cyber only with non-ugly people of your preferred gender – that's guaranteed!

Busy working   Oh no!   What to do?
No choice...   Fire in the hole!

Guaranteed to make your girlfriend happy FOR EVER!

Order

NEW!

Phone them up talk to them! Uses landline technology. Plugs into a wall! Yes the wall!

Order

BELOVED SPONSORS

I USED TO BE a REBEL but NOW I'M FAT and OLD CLOTHING CO.

SPECIALISTS IN:
outsized skater gear
leathery jackets
COATS WITH BITS OF FUR ON **THEM**

Make Your Own Blog!

HEADER

HEADER

TITLE

SUBTITLE

POSTS

PROFILE

Write your hesitant profile here

ARCHIVE

POSTS

BLOG

A blog is an online diary in which you pour observations, moans and groans, daily. They're really very readable. Everyone has one these days. So why be left out? You don't actually have to be able to write to keep a blog. Just use our cut-and-paste technology to compose your posts...

YOUR FIRST BLOG POST TEMPLATE

Well, [hello / hi / howdy] I guess this is my first blog entry. [Hello / Hi / Howdy] I'm not sure why I'm doing this, really, but all my [friends / colleagues / family members] seem to be doing it, so [here I am! / here I am! / here I am!] It should be fun, sharing all my [thoughts / ideas / memories] with all of you, and keeping you all up to date with my daily [life / activities / bowel issues] I wonder what you're [thinking / doing / feeling] reading this blog? Maybe tell me by commenting below? That would be [ace / great / wonderful] Oh the internet is so [ace / great / wonderful] I wonder what I should write? My brain has gone a bit [blank / empty / mushy] Er, my [mum / dad / sister] is going into hospital for a [hip replacement / heart bypass / ingrowing toenail] next week, and to tell you the truth I'm a bit [worried / happy / indifferent] about it. But I'm sure it will be ok. I'm running out of [things / stuff / news] to say on my first blog. Thank you all for reading, and don't forget to check back [soon / tomorrow / sometime] for more [fun / thrills / banality] Ole!

DAILY BLOG POST TEMPLATE

Have you seen what [chonkylips / plasticegg / God] has said about the [blogosphere / internet / blogonet] I just wasn't sure whether to [post it to / puke over / say 'pchtaw!' to] my [blog / cereal / self] That [guy / girl / blogger] is such a complete [genius / idiot / toss ladder] Here's a link to some [dancing kittens / pictures of prolapses / sermonising about Bush] Really good! Hey well I bet you've probably all [seen / yawned over / ignored] it already . Anyway please leave a comment! And whoever's been leaving [nasty comments / pictures of prolapses / spammage] in my inbox please stop.

LAST EVER BLOG POST TEMPLATE

This, I'm sad to say, is [without doubt / most likely / probably] going to be my last blog entry. I know I've said it [three / four / sixty] times before, but this time I mean it. Seriously. Please don't try to stop me. There are [three / four / sixty] reasons why I don't feel that i can go on. Firstly, it's difficult for me knowing that I've got [so many / so few / no] readers. I feel that the whole blogging thing is becoming [stressful / pointless / a tortured yet narcissitic cry for help] This blog is important to me but I need to devote more time to my [partner / personal hygiene / other blogs] My time spent telling you my secrets has also stopped me from doing important things such as [working / breathing / eating] I have found it so addictive, but stopping this blog NOW is a sacrifice I think I'm going to have to make. No! You can't stop me. I've really enjoyed sharing my [thoughts / hangups / low grade political insights] with you over the last few [months / weeks / hours] months, whoever you may be. See you [on the other side / around / er, tomorrow?]

033

REAL LIFE

JOIN NOW
MEMBERSHIP IS FREE

REAL LIFE IS A 3D
INTERACTIVE WORLD
CREATED AND OWNED BY SOME
OF ITS RESIDENTS.

- ❂ SPANS 6 CONTINENTS
- ❂ MANY SPECIES & ECONOMIES
- ❂ VERY REALISTIC GRAPHICS
- ❂ NO ELVES. NO TROLLS*

*some dwarves

FIRST 16 YEARS
SUBSCRIPTION FREE!
▶105

UNDER 18? WARNING ADULT CONTENT

QUOTES FROM THE PRESS

"Highly addictive. Very gritty. The 'end of the world' plot is fantastic." **TotalGameLord** ▶043

"Hmmmm, I found the physics a bit unrealistic." **Spodwire** ▶098

"If Civilisation and Grand Theft Auto had a love child – this would be it!" **PCSpod**

"Lovely! Beautiful! Yum!" **Gahooogle Good News** ◀017

Total Residents:	6,573,694
Logged In Last 60 Days:	6,573,604
Died In Last 60 secs:	22,812
US$ Spent:	$ 998,995,332,863,026
Another incomprehensible no:	445,489

beer in the morning noon and night

pubs
- browse by location
- browse by smell
- browse by fights
- browse by crampedness
- what pub?
- you like pub?
- top 4000

sort by extras
- crisps
- pickled eggs
- dartboard
- shove ha'penny
- jazz on Sundays
- dead people
- World Of Warcraft

general
- drunk?
- go on
- have another
- what are you, gay?
- go on, just one more
- thass my boy
- get it darn your neck

during the last month

- 227 pubs added to the site
- 2 new pubs visited
- 4342 pub comments by users
- 1212 new registered users

random quotes

"This place is run by idiots, frequented by idiots. They don't know how to change the barrels, all the regulars are either dribbling or singing nursery rhymes at each other. The pub quiz is a piece of piss. I win £50 every week, easy as you like."
KeepItLight

"Large pub, incorporating beer garden, restaurant, 50,000-seater football stadium, shopping mall, biscuit factory and several other pubs, but still very intimate."
N@velGaz0r

"It served Buddingworths Extra Grumpy which is a thumbs up. They had pork lips behind the bar - another thumb up - and a huge pile of free Jap scat so three thumbs up!"
BloodyWomen

top ten pubs

The CTRL V and CTRL P
Barracuda Gdns, Gt.Stafford - see full details
This is a crime ridden hellhole with precious little to recommend it. My wife went to the toilet and found the word "scum" written on the door in blood. During a single evening I was defrauded by the fruit machine, threatened by the landlord and anally assaulted at the bar. Aside that, it was a reasonably romantic evening. **Darren**

The Prince Of Gydanskiy Poluostrov
The Glebe, Little Maddesden, Bucks see full details
One gastro makeover too far. Five waiters guided us to our table, which was bedecked with lilies and other assorted flora. Each individual French fried potato arrived in its own wooden sheath, and a flaxen haired maiden flounced around us, bearing a flagon of sauce bearnaise and whispering "I will now adorn your steak." The bill came to £123.50, I only wanted a pint. **MollyBloom**

The Phimosis & Firkin
Calthorpe Industrial Estate, Harlesdon, NW10 - see full details
Christ, this place is filthy. It's like a skip. You can't move for empty crisp packets, newspapers, broken glass and cigarette butts. The carpet's damp, and the stench when you walk in is foul. My beer had hairs in it, and there was a tooth in my girlfriend's wine. I don't think anyone even bothers going to the toilets, they just sit in their own filth. Fantastic jukebox, though – Elvis Costello! All the albums! Ace. **KeepItLight**

The Mobile & Charger
5 Louche Terrace, Haughty St, Hoxton, EC1 - see full details
Is it a bar? Is it a pub? This bizarre pub-themed bar looks like a pub, but I think it's a bar. I asked if it was a pub, and the bartender laughed at me. Pub-lovers will love the pubbiness of this bar, while bar lovers will appreciate the weirdness of a chic bar that looks exactly like a pub. Unless you can appreciate several dozen levels of irony simultaneously, don't go here. I'm really confused. **Kathryn Merchant**

The F*** & C***
98 Stabbings Road, Weybrige - see full details
I like a pub with a bit of an edge to it, but this was terrifying. When I walked in there was a terrifying silence, and everybody turned and stared at me. It stayed exactly like that until the moment I left 4 hours later. The clientele included 2 bare-knuckle boxers, 12 dogs and a transvestite bingo caller called "Stefan". The only booze available was 2-litre bottles of White Lightning. Grim. **Scaramungous**

The Point & Click
5 HTTP Terrace, London - see full details
Initially impressive, but has its limitations. The image was stable on a 1080i signal, and had the fewest scaling artifacts of any display at that resolution. But pronounced, scrolling horizontal bands made viewing awkward, not to mention the problems with de-interlacing, colour tracking and smearing on moving images. Avoid. **Johnathon**

Gaybar, Amersham
Bareback Leisure Complex, Hulme, Mancs - see full details
Me and my wife Helen were shocked to see the transformation of the old Wagon & Horses public house, where we have spent many happy summer evenings. Where once there was a pool table, there is now a group of gyrating homosexuals. Where once there was a salad cart, there is another group of gyrating homosexuals. My question: why all the homosexuals? **Anon**

books about pubs

PUBS of DEEPEST AFRICA
the best-selling guide
buy from amasszone.com

BUILD YOUR OWN PUB
have it up before closing time
buy from amasszone.com

MR PUB
for young drinkers

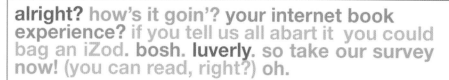
alright? how's it goin'? your internet book experience? if you tell us all abart it you could bag an iZod. bosh. luverly. so take our survey now! (you can read, right?) oh.

▶131

PROPERTY SEARCH

narrow your criteria to the maxx

min beds
min price
min neighbours
min hidden flaws
min thinness of walls
min quality of door handles

SEARCH NOW

HOME MORTAGE FAQ

Common questions posed by visitors to this site.

- How much can i borrow?
- How much do I pay back?
- Over how long?
- Sorry I thought you said over two decades. Hah.
- You were kidding right?
- What?
- What about global warming FFS?

PROPERTIES: Just on the market

Worcester Mews, Mayfair, London W1
Sumptuous lower-ground floor castle. 18 cloakrooms, miles of corridors, state of the art doorhandles, mirror maze, dark room, Star Trek transporters (prototypes). Timewasters, gawkers and couples on a public sex dare welcome. **£6.5m.**

PROPERTIES: Out of your league

The Perineum, Sebastopol Drive, Virginia Water, Berks
Spectacularly spacious family home. Five bedrooms, three further bedrooms, more bedrooms and another bedroom, all with direct access to a Museum Of Bedrooms via fur-lined subway system. £4.8m.

Pudenda Crescent, Brighton, W Sussex
Exquisite eighth-time buy. Vertical, south-facing garden, Sky-facing roof, ultra-secure visitors' holding bay podule and rather nice shoe rack. A snip at £5.2m.

Evergreen Sq, Hampstead Garden Suburb, London N2
Staggeringly gigantic palace suiting energetic newly-weds. 12-hour porterage alternating with 12-hour burglary opportunities. Parking for 120 cars, sunny terrace, rainy kitchen. £18.3m.

Vainglorious Passage, Wilmslow, Cheshire
Period property perfect for a person. Antique wood boiler, foil-coated Media Room, escalator, central atrium full of shops and restaurants. Yours for just £2,999,995.

PROPERTIES: First time buyers

The Monkey Hutch, Dog Kennel Hill, SE22
Small cramped kennel-like structure used to breed simians. Wall-mounted lifeforms, rolled edge effluent stack, plus a door, window, cupboard, sink and hole (toilet). Chain free. £21,000

Jizz Sluice, 80 Lube Alley, Soho
Charming and secluded section of internal pumbing underneath a sex show. Spacious enough to accommodate a couple, lying down. Easy walking distance to some coin-operated Toss Booths and some neon. £249,000

Half House, Falluja
Contemporary demi-maisonette in desirable locale. Split, gas, space, glazed. Needs some walls. Early other property viewing highly recommended. Now half price: £79,950.

19 Arnsdale Way, Central London
Ex-council gun turret on the famous Abaddon Estate which has seen extensive renovation and razing by the local residents. Off-street moat, stainless steel portcullis, and marble-effect slits. Chain free. £99,950

FEATURES

Paint It White
A weekly guide to transforming your home and getting the best possible price for it by only using endless 5-litre pots of nearly-white paint. This week's colour: Milky Thighs

Win! Win! Win!
Your chance to win your very own gift-wrapping room, perfect for storing all your scissors, sellotape and wrapping paper.

Lofty Ambitions
Convert your loft into a loft. Convert your swimming pool into a loft. A watery one. Anyway lofts are in!

ON TV TODAY

Only The Best For Me
The number of rejected properties hits 32 this week, as aspirational pedants Joy and Pete sneer at a skirting board that doesn't quite live up to their expectations.
CBBC 2.40pm

Do You Know Who We Are?
More of the De Lusignan family's thrilling race to displace a local community by buying up an entire Slovenian village on the cheap.
Discovery Home & Leisure, 8pm

This One Will Be The One
Tear-soaked men and women pray that this house will be the one to make them feel complete and happy and ALIVE.
All channels.

 **You Flue**

Home | Videos | Distractions | FlimFlam | Flotsam | Jetsam

Browse

Most Recent
Most Illegal
Most Horrible
Most Boring
Most Japanese

Category

Poorly conceived
mashups
Dogs & Cats
Fuglies
Chicks (hot)
Chicks (less hot)
Show offs
Narcissists
Fights
Films About Farts

Featured Videos   See More Videos

The International Spam Film Festival
05:21
An incredible world festival of short films inspired by real spam emails. Watch the award-winning thriller "You Loan Request Approved", the romcom "She Will Be Surprised What Happened WIth You Dick", quixotic sci-fi in "PHxatARMCY", Arthouse number "Maoron Be Grunt Inbreeding" and the Dsylexic Dsylexian nightmare "Funon A Betetr Suotloin".

Tags: Vialis Ciagra OEM Red Hot Stocks Nymphets Czech Teens Cum Pill woodland iDiploma Argyll Scotland Cheap MEds Replica Watches

Added: 3 months ago in Category: Entertainment
From: chainsawcraft
Views: 56,693
★★★½☆
556 ratings

Best Of Star War fan films
05:21
In a galaxy not so far, far away are some of the best pro-amateur Star War inspired films Including "*Bone Washing Lucas*", "*I Spunked My Parents College Funds On This Trite 2 Minute Homage To Some Kids Film From The 70s*", the gritty award-winning *EastEndors*, animated feature *Ewok's Up Doc*, and the full feature-length green-screened fan film, Episode VIII: *A New Coat*.

EPISODE VIII: A NEW COAT

Tags: Sad Sad Sad Sad Sad

Added: 2 months ago in Category: Entertainment
From: BuboeFett
Views: 9,575,322,298,111,113
★★½☆☆
90000000 ratings

The Best UFO Footage EVER (fuzzy)
04:43
Added: 2 months ago
From: Area52
Views: 83,999
★★½☆☆
8 ratings

man beheaded - totally awesomely decapitation NSFW
02:18
Added: 2 months ago1 day ago
From: nirarbel
Views: 83,926
★★½☆☆
135 ratings

What HAppens when I fart a lot in public
02:16
Added: 1 week ago
From: airbiscuit
Views: 8,964,787
★★★★★★★
★★★★★★★
135 ratings

Mentos Eating Jap Scat Kittens Driving Monster Trucks On Tatooine
01:46
Added: 2 months ago1 day ago
From: navymrgoodbar
Views: 77,087
★★½☆☆

Still of hot chick to make you click (clip does not include chick)
04:23
Added: 2 months ago1 day ago
From: Laughing4Ever
Views: 75,204
★★½☆☆
43 ratings

ã‚·ã f£ã f©ã f ã f¯ ã€€à¤ªã¤‚ã‚‚ã‚·ã fž ã ffã‚¡ã f¼ã‚‚
04:33
Added: 2 months ago1 day ago
From: TheRealParis
Views: 70,640
★★½☆☆
338 ratings

My Ex-Wife And Me At It At Home In Bed Take That Sara
00:16
Added: 2 months ago22 hours ago
From: DarrenMarshall04
Views: 57,715
★★½☆☆
19 ratings

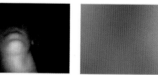
My Ex-Wife And Me At It At Home In Bed 2 Sara I Hope You See This You Have Killed Me
06:35
Added: 2 months ago1 day ago
From: DarrenMarshall04
Views: 55,693
★★½☆☆
15 ratings

Pages: 1 | 2 | 3 | 4 | 5 | Next

YouFlue
About
How much money?   Yes
                   That much

Help & Info
Go out
Look at the sky

Breathe The Air
Listen for birds

Catch a neighbour's eye
Scuttle back inside

You Flue

Home | **Videos** | **Sportoids** | **Jerks** | **YearBookers** | **Scaries**

» Most Viewed
Time
» Today
This Hour
This Second
Now
And Now
And Now
And Now

Category
» All
Farts & Intestinal Humour
Cars Crashing & Flipping
Comedy: Actually Talented
People
Lame Acoustic Covers
Stoned Girls
Drunk Pets
Ah God
Is This What It's
All About

Cool Executions! Clown Hangs while Still Smiling
04:43
Added: 2 months ago
From: keepitlight
Views: 84,787
★★★★★
135 ratings

Hi! I'm Angela from Arabia or somewhere!
02:18
Added: 1 month ago
From: vamptress
Views: 943,122
★★★★★
135 ratings

My tribute to Tokyo Ritz with all new footage I made myself
02:18 [▶040]
Added: 1 month ago
From: ilovetokyo
Views: 943,122
★★★★★
135 ratings

Funny Cat On Trampline
01:46
Added: 4 years ago
From: lowbrown
Views: 999
★★★★★
135 ratings

Amazing! Man eats own head. Totally geuine.
04:23
Added: 2 months ago
From: Laughing4Ever
Views: 75,204
★★★☆☆
43 ratings

Kittens Skitter Uncontrollably On Lino Before Hitting Uncovered Industrial Fans!
04:33
Added: 2 months ago
From: TheRealParis
Views: 70,640
★★★☆☆
338 ratings

StayPlation 360 unpacked by 3 year old beatboxing robo-breakdancer.
02:18
Added: 1 month ago
From: scaramangous
Views: 943,122
★★★★★

Yummy Mummy wearing bright flees skateboarding on a child's buggy board gets lanced on victorian railing so the barb sticks out of her back. Ewwwww! SFW
06:35
From: DarrenMarshall04
Views: 55,693
★★★☆☆

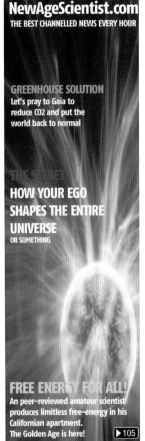

Teenager fucked up on mum's vodka stash mates with family Schnauser while mates jeer
04:43
Added: 2 months ago
From: lilscrappy
Views: 84,787
★★★☆☆

OMFG man sticks bowling ball up his goddamn nose. Totally genuine.
02:18
Added: 2 months ago
From: nirarbel
Views: 83,926
★★★☆☆
135 ratings

Me screwing my soon to be ex-wife front of a mirror. Enjoy her. I did. While it lasted.
02:18
Added: 1 month ago
From: darrenmarshall
Views: 943,122 [▶085]

Hot Girl despairing at people only valuing her for her hotness (episode 903)
01:46
Added: 2 months ago
From: navymrgoodbar
Views: 77,087
★★★☆☆

Amputee Juggling With Chainsaws episode 2 (he never learns)
04:23
Added: 2 months ago
From: Laughing4Ever
Views: 75,204
★★★☆☆
43 ratings

Polish Animation (two Balls of Plasticine Meet And Then Roll Away)
04:33
Added: 2 months ago
From: TheRealParis
Views: 70,640
★★★☆☆
338 ratings

content removed

Brilliant! Dock Of the Bay sung Entirely in Esperanto By Two Gay Chinese Guys in Man U Tops
00:16
Added: 2 months ago
From: TrashManky
Views: 57,715
★★★☆☆
19 ratings

Iran's Secret Mentos Facility (leaked DOD footage)
06:35
Added: 2 months ago
From: Johnathon [▶102]
Views: 55,693
★★★☆☆
15 ratings

YouFlue
Wow
You're Rich!

Yes
We Are

Help & Info
Pick Up The Phone
Who To Ring?

Not her
Not him!

Who then?
No one

039

You **Flue**

Search for [   ] [Search]

Tokyo Ritz - SpankTasm

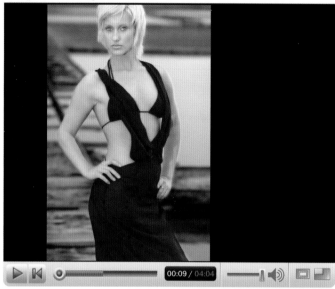

00:09 / 04:04

Added **December 24**
From ilovetokyo

[✓ SUBSCRIBE]

its the video for Tokyo AMAZING new song (more)

Category Music

Tags Shit

URL http://www.youflue.com/watch?v=2Ju_FR1a8

Embed <object quality="0" viral potential="1"><para

Related | More from this user | Playlists

Showing 1-20 of about 12,300   See All Videos

Hairless child prodigy playing the guitar better than Santana
03:00
Views: 92069

Me Using The Comp To Film Me With My Computer OMG 03:00
From: noclip
Views: 9

Football 10 Best Legs Twisted at Grey Faced Angle 03:00
From: iluvgravy
Views: 92069

Joe Makes Video Response To Sarah Video About Joe's Video Response - About Time!!!
91:03

Only Fools & Horses Del Falls Through Bar L0Lz0r
00:21
From: bbc
Views: 432,724,996,007,501.3

Showing 1-20 of about 12,300   See All Videos

Rate this video:
★★★☆☆
14 ratings

♥ Fall in Love
👥 Wipe Your Face
✉ Put in letter
📧 Send to gran
✖ Flag as watchable

Views: **6,734** | Comments: **5** | Favorited: **26** times

Comments & Responses

Post a video response
Post a text comment

buckley155 (1 month ago)
this is a shot-ot song love it
(Reply) (Spam)

37lambs (3 weeks ago)
Great song, but i wudnt call it a video its a fcukin picture!
(Reply) (Spam)

rikkuknight (2 weeks ago)
thanks for posting; this is one of my favorite songs :D
(Reply) (Spam)

piinkxprincessxx (4 days ago)
love the song but what the hell with like one pic??
(Reply) (Spam)

thedarkcourtsjester (3 days ago)
No sound and one pic FFS! This book internet thing sucks. Im getting my money back.
(Reply) (Spam)

Comment on this video
Post a video response

[   ] [Post Comment]

YouFlue
Buy Us A Drink? No
Lend us a- No!

Help & Info
Gone Dark Now Spoken To No One
All Day Apart From Myself
And the Flies

Copyright © 2006 YouFlue, Inc. YouFlue.com is a Bahoogle.com company

040

TUESDAY 19TH NOVEMBER

10 Things You Can Do To Stop Global Warming NOW

It's not a definite list by any means but it's a good starting point for those of us trying to do better. The full list in wallchart form can be bought from us for $100 dollars

1. **Act Now** And hide under the bed
2. **Become Aware** Say "shit shit shit" several times after reading a terrifying news report and then turn on the TV.
3. **Information Is Power** Burn hours of energy surfing the web for green sites epousing energy saving ideas.
4. **Cool It** Make a lot of ice.
5. **On Second Thoughts** No, no - don't make a lot of ice. That's really bad.
6. **Drive With No Tyres** It's surprisingly easy to reduce emissions when you're not burning rubber
7. **Recycle Yourself** Your belching fat ass is going to generate tonnes of carbon per annum. Why not jump into a carbon sink instead?
8. **Move Your Thermostat Onto The Ceiling** Harder to reach. Harder to turn up. Works with cakes too, if you're dieting.
9. **Handglide To Overseas Meetings** Zero energy costs. 100% danger
10. **Use More Water** Sea levels are rising so let's get drinking the stuff!

posted by SoftWear | 06.23am | 12 comments

WEDNESDAY 20TH NOVEMBER

Oh Tom On!

Did you know there used to be 16 million different species of tomato? Now there's just one, a perfect round one that's nearly completely tasteless. Don't stand for it. Demand these long-forgotten varieties from your grocer or order from us. Only $400 per lb.

Pissentilt

Chonky's chonk

Andat Warty Mellon

Bakino Fazo

Lady's Knuckles

Chernobyl Dobber

WEDNESDAY 20TH NOVEMBER

Emperor Penguin!

This oversized egg is central to the astonishing mating ritual of the emperor penguin. Once laid, the egg is transferred by the female to the male without ever touching the ground. If the egg is exposed to the frozen Arctic ground for more than a few seconds, the unborn chick inside will die. It is tended to by its father for four months, during which time males huddle together to protect the eggs in temperatures below -62 degrees centigrade. Their only source of water is the snow that falls around them. Anyway, it makes a enormous bloody nice-tasting omelette. Order yours today from us for just $59 each.

posted by SoftWear | 5.12pm | 96 comments

WEDNESDAY 20TH NOVEMBER

Just Corking!

Because cork is stripped from bark without needing to fell trees, it's the material of the future. Cork makes a great insulator, floor tile, spliff roach and mobile phone cover. And if we may say, it also makes a damn prophalactic! (just like in the olden days)

posted by SoftWear | 06.41pm | 1 comments

Hey! There! I'm Candy. Welcome to my humble eco blog

Here I keep track of all the latest ways you can help save the planet. The best way to do this I've found is by buying the worthwhile things that I sell. Since my Crystals4Business shop shut down, I've been harnessing the power of the web to give my healing energy to the world. 2% off all first purchases.

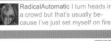

📶 **RSS ECO News Headlines**
• Red Sky In The Morning Sign Of Imminent Danger, say Sheep Herders
• Why Rednecks Need Higher Factor Sun Cream
• More Cyclists Die Than Live
• Official: Sun Causes Global Warming

Blogroll
• Gorillas In The Shit
• CO2 Funhaus
• Compact Flourescent Lightbulb Review

The Depression Session

Cheer up - it's not *all* bad!

"Scientific studies have shown that plane travel is, per capita, the most polluting form of transport possible. But only very successful Western people travel by plane. Most of the pollution blows away onto central Asia, India and Africa where people are too poor to notice. Hurrah!"

Have similar guilt-relieving missives emailed to you everyday.
▶096

Sportobix

daily bites of sport for people who don't actually do any

HOME | KICKING | HITTING | THROWING | CHASING | VROOMING

ATHLETICS

VULKOV WITHDRAWS DUE TO GROIN INJURY

Bulgarian shotput champion Ivan Vulkov has abandoned gold medal hopes in the European Athletic Championships following a repeat of the groin injury he sustained last year.

TENNIS

STRESS BLAMED FOR MIRO'S FRENCH OPEN EXIT

Tim Miro conceded defeat in his quarter final of the French Open yesterday, as his coach blamed the intense pressure Miro has endured after recent tournament failures

BOXING

DIY DISASTER MAKES ROBERTS THE UNDERDOG

A routine afternoon of DIY culminated in a series of cataclysmic electric shocks for Herbie Roberts, leaving him barely in the running for tonight's light welterweight clash with Joey Burrito.

MOTORSPORT

BROKEN HEART ENDS GARDEN'S RACE

Grand Slam contender Willis Garden quit the starting grid today, blaming a broken heart. The young driver, was apparently the victim of a random chucking last night from a girl he met on the internet.

DARTS

SVARGOORD OUT OF ACTION AFTER MAGIC TRICK

Reigning World Darts Champion, Kart Svargood dislocated his shoulder today when trying to tear a phone book in half for a kid's magic show. The jinxed show had earlier seen the tip of a child's finger severed when a guillotine trick went badly wrong.

RUGBY

MALNUTRITION BLAMED FOR ALL BLACKS DEFEAT

After a 53-3 mauling at the hands of Wales, captain Ross Armitage blamed liver spots and bleeding mucous membranes due to a lack of orange juice intake during training.

MOTORSPORT

F1 CATASTROPHE PUTS FORMULAS 2 & 3 IN DRIVING SEAT

A multiple pile-up at the Hungaroring leaves all but one of this season's Formula One competitors with severe frontal lobe damage and in a state of akinetic mutism; Frenchman Jean Letroux escapes with a broken nail.

SWIMMING

ARMSTRONG HITS BACK OVER 'DRUG SMEARS'

Beleaguered diving champ Kurt Armstrong today responded to rumours he will fail a drug test in the press by picking up a nearby dustbin and throwing it at reporters. Witnesses said he then rolled on the floor shouting "I am Jesus, I am the centre of the universe, Come lie with me."

GOLF

MCGINTY DECAPITATION SCOTCHES US MASTERS HOPE

A grisly neck injury while approaching the 11th hole at the Augusta National left defending Masters champion Jez McGinty struggling at 2 over par and his head hanging off by a tendon.

FOOTBALL

UKRAINIAN SIDE DECIMATED BY SPACE-BORN ANDROMEDA STRAIN

Ukraine's entire squad has been crippled by a vicious extra-terrestrial virus that has baffled doctors in Kiev. As they mutate into bestial lifeforms, we assess the prospects for the human race.

---

3 Word Headlines

- Ball Kicked Hard
- Slough Might Win
- Caught Off Hat
- Big Defeat Wednesday
- Morning Has Broken
- Like First Morning
- Drugs Drugs Drugs
- Trophy In Bag
- Come On Then
- Blackbird has Spoken
- Team Wins Game
- Man Drops Ball
- Expected Outcome Occurs
- Results Prompt Indifference
- Fan Eats Pie
- This Just In
- Headline Writer Sacked

Latest Headlines

Conkers from Maidstone: Vinegar Dave beats Boy Boysey

The Weakest Link: Anne Templeford is the weakest link, goodbye

Pub Clash Saturday: Kings Arms Teddington thrashes The Butchers Fletch in a fight

Fishing from Reykyavik: 22,425 fish

Siberian Iceball: Saskylakh −42oC Udachnyy −23oC

Tennis: Meerkamp beats Ulrich with the underside of his racket 6-2 6-4 7-6

Latest Score: Sport 0:Drugs 4

Poll!

Do you like sport?
- ⦿ yes!
- ◯ no!
- ◯ sometimes!

TOTALGAMELORD

KILL EVERYBODY

YOUR MISSION: TO DESTROY THE ENTIRE WORLD!
BUT carefully and strategically so you don't run out of cash to buy the bombs and weapons to do the job.

PONG 2007

OLD GAMES MADE NEW!
3D graphics & up to 32 player online PongFrenzy™ - "WTF!" PC Spod

Latest & Greatest

About | See More ⌄

Clan Manager 2008
Manage the egos and appointments for your online gaming clan

Trolls and Guns
Trolls With Guns. Elves With Lasers. Damn. This game's got everything.

The Ultimate Survival Horror
Can you survive the 31st December on the streets of a British town?

Latest News

World War II: Most Horrible Battles
Relive the gruesome horror of World War II from your office chair. Armed with just a pistol you take on artillery and armoured machine gun emplacements. Cry out for your mother as you're shorn in two. But don't worry - *there's plenty more where you came from.*
Not a single penny goes to veteran organisations

Mac vs PC:
Settle the historic battle once and for all. Hordes of brushed titanium robots versus beige or fashionably black ones.

StreetFighter: Philosopher Edition
Nietzche versus Plotinus. Sartre takes on Derrida. Foucault headbutts Hegel.

You STARTIN?

It's you versus a series of world class diplomats and spiritual leaders. You must use all your moves to provoke them into fighting you. **Moves:** Whatever, The Nipple Tweak, Genital Flash. **Enemies:** Mother Theresa, Aung San Suu Kyi, & George Foreman.

Nofriendo
REMOTE CONTROL HERO

Master all 358 buttons on all 16 of your remotes. Get your TV, VCR, DVR, Cable Box, XBox, PSII, Stereo, MD all working simultaneously.

Real Life ◄ 034
The massively multiplayer online role playing game. Now with over 6 billion users.

Picks | Previews | Reviews | Videos | Features

Metal Gear Chugger
Rove the streets of a metropolis creeping up on strangers and trapping them into a yearly subscription for Amnesty International by *whatever means necessary*. Respond chirpily no matter what the provocation. Dodge insults, fists and bullets. Start in Milton Keynes, work your way up to London, then New York then the final challenge, Iraq. Yes, can you survive as a white Western drama student on the streets of Bahgdad? *"A dreary soul-sapping game."* PC Spod.

Sim Insurgency
Kick out the oppressors by any means necessary. And your fellow countrymen who are slightly different to you. And anyone who gets caught in the cross fire. *"The narcissism of minor differences has never been so much fun"* PC Spod

Park Football Evolution
Experience the thrills and spills of after-school football in astounding realism. Features: 17-18 a side, infinite wings, goal hangers, a fat kid nobody wants, and a selection of over 20 different jumpers for goal posts. Now with new "That Was In. No It Wasn't" beat'em up sub-game. *"Dangerous."* PC Spod

Sid Meyer's Sid Meyer
From the unrivalled master of simulation games comes the ultimate simulation game. You play game guru Sid Meyer who's got to create a game about game guru Sid Meyer creating a game about Sid Meyer. Arrrghh. Stop it. *"FFS!"* PC Spod

Naked Wars II: Tunnel Through The Ring
This magicky real-time strategy game features all your favourite adversaries - monsters, elves and trolls - all naked, oiled up and shiny as f**k. Features: tunnels, rings, tight squeezes, and lots of bending down to pick up the artefacts, mercenaries with their tops off, sailors, and long haired warriors with great big swords. *"I stayed up all night playing it. I love the smell of gay palms in the morning."* PC Spod

Gun Shop
You're trapped in a gun shop. Only one option. You're gonna have to shoot your way out. This blood-soaked first person shooter uses the RenderGore engine v4.0 which boasts: intestinal shrapnel, BrainSpatter particle system, and super realistic musculo-skeletal shred rendering.

Games for Old People

Granny Turismo
The Million Selling Octogenarian racer
Pilot your Allegro round 10 city centres at over 6 to 7 miles an hour. **Boost** your speed with betablockers. **Upgrade** to bifocals. But watch out for the colostomy slick! **Compete** in the Gran Prix for The Cup (of tea) or go for the ultimate prize: a pack of Scottish Shortcakes and a Brompton Cocktail.

Try these other oldie games:

grans swift autopsy | always winter nights | QUAKING | BACKSEAT DRIVER

FROM JAPANESE GAMES LEGEND USHURI USHURI

WHAT?
GO DEVIL INSIDE LEGEND

"We waited for the English version and even when that came it was still incomprehensible" PCSpod

Windows The Game
Manage your files and try to stop Windows World from crashing, **Don't let the Blue Screen Of Death get you!**
"Excellent. Trains kids for a lifetime of using Mucrosoft products". PCSpod.com

---

Worldwide | **About Us** | **TotalGameLord.com** is totally pwned by **Bahoogle.com**

justByou.co.uk
for the modern woman

| Shopping | Shopping | Shopping | Shopping | Shopping | Shopping | Shopping | Shopping | Shopping |

justbyou yousletter

[SIGN UP]

view all yousletters

features
Secret lives, true confessions

Bingegasm
My name is Sarah and last week I bought an entire bargain bucket of chicken thighs from KCF.

True life trauma stories

I Went Into The Men's Toilets
Bleeeeeeeeeeeeeee! I didn't plan it. I was drunk. I made a mistake, one I'll regret for the rest of my life...

highlights

Diet
Change eating forever
Try Calista's new foodless recipes.

Interiors
Get the latest look
Transform your home but not yourself.

Shopping
The best bargains
Where to shop, when to shop, how to shop.

Self-help
Breathe breathe!
Yoga techniques for when the shops are closed.

Love & Sex
10 ways...
To please your man while he's having sex with someone else.

True Stories
Hooked!
I'm addicted to stories about addiction to scratchcards.

Beauty
Complexion Perfection
Achieve flawless skin with four layers of foundation.

Lifestyle
How to cheat at poker
A silly game with so many silly rules.

forums

What you're talking about right now...

Why are men's nipples so rubbish?

Someone tried to take my storecard. I lammed them.

My husband's saggy nutsack. How I learned to love it.

My mother-in-law just died. Black is sooooo last season. What should I wear to the funeral?

Carbon Dioxide levels are at their highest since the Cambrian era. What should I wear?

Which would you rather be? Fat or dead?

Going down KCF for a binge. What should I wear?

His best friend's guest towel is grey. Should I dump him?

I just laid an egg. Is that right?

He hasn't called for a year. What does that mean?

How many times should I say *meh* in a day?

What colours are you wearing RIGHT NOW?

And what about now?

A good relationship with a coprophiliac - does it ever work?

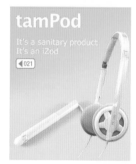

| Select Site ▾ | | justbyou.co.uk ▾ |

justByou.co.uk
for the modern woman

wrinkled ears? try...AUROX XL
you're just three painful injections away from youthful ears

| Eating | Feeling Guilty | Vomiting | Eating | Feeling Guilty | Vomiting | Eating | Feeling Guilty | Etc |

latest on the blogs

This year's looks
The latest accoutrement from the world's catwalks.

skimasks   legwarmers around the waist   stilts   glow in the dark gums

posted by Katie 04:13am

This season, last season
Keep your look fresh with a few well chosen updates.

slapheads: "in"

LAST YEAR	THIS YEAR
Jeans tucked into boots	Jeans over boots
Long deep handbags	Longer deeper handbags
Little black dress	Huge white dress
Pointy toes	Frostbitten toes
Big hair	No hair

posted by Katie 04:18am

Horoscope

"If today is your birthday, don't be surprised if a few cards drop through your letterbox. Today could be the day when everyone showers you with attention. Who knows, you might even have your cake and eat it!"

posted by Madame Femto 05:20am

Top Bulimia hints
What's the best way to handle your eating disorder? We asked the forumites last week. (Hi! You guys!). Well, here's the top voted tip: "Start off with carrots. That way you know when you've gotten rid of everything"..
posted by Madame Femto 06:15am

Internal Affirmations

You're out with the girls. Everything's a bit slurry. Time to be strong. I write these little affirmations on piece of card in my purse so I don't end up embarrassing myself - again!

Don't like companies testing your makeup on animals?

Not a problem...

Home Cosmetic Testing Kit

CONTENTS: swabs, control group acids petri dish, cotton wool, disposal sack and housebrick

EMERGENCY?

Dying of an overdose?
DIAL 944
Our expert team of cleaners will come round and tidy your house so the pictures look nice in the local paper

tags

alcohol aaah aaah apostrophes (correct use of) axe murderers baby body clock broody binge bored boring boring men chatting chips chocolate cravings cancer carrots cunnilingus divorce despair dating diazepam food frenzy guilt gym gym guilt hangover lipo loneliness love loneliness love loneliness love LOVE marriage men motherfuckers lush green orchid musk party pretty girls passive aggression projection pomegranite persimmon pumpkin puffy eyes plucking purge relationships rose petals rinse sex spontaneous spirit of amber tia maria unloved vibrator vibrator wounds wax wine yoga zzzzzzzz

THE ANTI-DIET DIET
the sensational new diet fad from America!
swap
• pilates for chapatis
• situps for fry-ups
• your daily run for a daily bun
FIND OUT MORE

i don't know why i'm bloody laughing!
i just am

extrascentsory perception
the new range
SUDDENLY AGAINST THE FRIDGE
Cold Dark Stranger

| Select a site ▼ | | justbyou.co.uk ▼ |

Schmapple Store

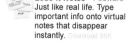
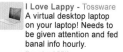
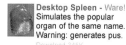
Final Act Pro 5

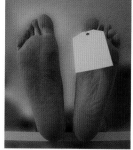

Euthanasia and suicide has never been so easy - or stylish. Packed with innovative features, Final Act Pro delivers a stunning solution for those wishing to resolve their end-life issues with efforless panache. Put the FUN back into Funeral.

Select your product:

●	**Single User**	**$79.00**
○	**Family Pack**	**$99.00**
○	**Cult Pack** (2-50 users)	**$9999.00**

New Features

Enjoy blazing performance and keyframe control over your death.

Use photocasting to share images of your passing with others over the internet.

Savour a range of death rites in a variety of languages and degrees of solemnity.

Create a pro-quality suicide note in a dazzling array of styles.

Diecast™ your final words and noises to a potential audience of millions with just one click.

Lighten the mood with radio-style jingles and sound bursts. Or give a gritty urban feel with our FuneralBeats(tm) add-on pack!

★★★★☆ **Based on 338 reviews**

Ex-Customer Reviews   See more >

Sort by [Newest ▼]   << first < prev | **1** | 2 | 3 | 4 | 5 | 6 | 7 | 8 | 9 | 10 | next > last >>

★★★★☆
Couldn't die without it
Written by LW from Wellington, New Zealand
November 14, 2006

I wanted to kill myself without embarrassing my wife and children. Final Act allowed me to do that and much much more. It even allowed me to write this 4 star review *post humously*. Nice one. ... Read more >

(7 of 13 people found this review useful)

Was this useful? (Yes) (No)   Report this as inappropriate >

★★★★★
Great despite some shortcomings
Written by CG from Cincinnati
November 14, 2006

I LOVE THIS ! This package has served me very well all the way to the end. That being said, Final Act Pro has some pretty major shortcomings. There is no undo button, for example. ... Read more >

(9 of 11 people found this review useful)

Was this useful? (Yes) (No)   Report this as inappropriate >

★★★★★
Gnnnnnaarrrrrrrghhhhhh!
Written by SM from Austria
November 13, 2006

gyaaargh........nurrr...ak....gott...in...himmel..... Read more >
[this Diecast™ sent by final act pro]
(1 of 19 people found this review useful)

Was this useful? (Yes) (No)   Report this as inappropriate >

Sort by [Obsequiousness ▼]   << first < prev | **1** | 2 | 3 | 4 | 5 | 6 | 7 | 8 | 9 | 10 | next > last >>

DreamOn Pro
Become a professional musician. In an instant.

Kill hours and hours of your free time believing that this single piece of good-looking software is your key to stardom. Then, after months of fiddling, end up with something that sounds exactly like it was stolen wholesale from someone way more talented than you. Three years ago.

- Make music, soundtracks and beats in full studio quality 48-bit surround
- Tinker endlessly
- Get nowhere

simulates every detail of
a real home studio

Squander this amazing creative power
Our innovative software instruments and plugins will keep you refining and refining and remixing and remixing for years

Shiny Shiny
No matter how bad your tunes are, the Excellentaliser will polish them up.

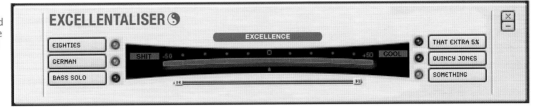

Fine Tune
We're not actually sure what this one does yet. But it has unlimited parameter adjustment!

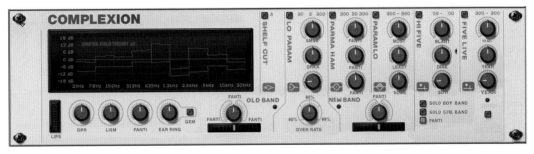

Tub Thumper
Emulates the shuddering rhythms of famously poor time keepers

Gotta Split
Shreds the unified band sound and attempts to stick it back together in time for album release.

Wear with pride
Gay beats to make it rain men on the dance floor.

Flattery
Imitate your favourite band at the touch of a button.

NEW! Paint It Black If your mix is just too white...

NEW! Wannabe Obscurity to fame and back again

Bored Pilots?

So this is what pilots get up to when they're waiting for their slot. Remind me never to fly NullAir again!

📄 9th Mar by DeathAngel   💬 Comments (20)   🌐 View in Bahoogle Earth

Categories: Identified Flying Objects, Skipping, and Tomfoolery

Mixed Messages

Ok you want to do some graffiti. You want to rage against the machine. Or articulate whatever is the prejudice de jour in your tinpoke town. But c'mon - think before you ink.

📄 9th Mar by Johnathon   💬 Comments (20)   🌐 View in Bahoogle Earth

Categories: Dumb Ass, Homophobia and Animals

The World Blowjob Competition

It took us a while to work out what this huge snaking queue of people were waiting for. Then, after some GPS cross-referencing and a lot of internet research, we worked it out. Famed pornstar Bubbles Malvoisin was attempting to fellate a record-breaking 612 men in under 12 hours. She managed 405. Unlucky girl!

📄 9th Mar by EdwinLecter   💬 Comments (8913)   🌐 View in Bahoogle Earth

Categories: Nasty

The Jaws Of Death

We'll let you work out what's going on here.

📄 9th Mar by Flipper   💬 Comments (20)   🌐 View in Bahoogle Earth

Categories: Flesh-eating, Dumb Animals and Fish

Action Movie Denouement

From this sateillite photo, it looks to us like a renegade cop who doesn't play by the rules has tracked down an evil drug / uranium / gold ingots smuggler to his dock-side hideaway. The hero's kidnapped family seems to have been rescued and now the hero is chasing the baddie down to avenge the death of his wife in a previous incident thought to be unrelated to this one.

- hero
- baddie
- hero's hot headed sidekick
- baddie's no 1 henchman (blonde one)
- mound for hero to throw himself on when the whole place goes up
- hero's feisty cop girlfriend
- baddies' female martial arts sidekick of questionnable sexuality

9th Mar by DeathAngel   Comments (20)   View in Bahoogle Earth

Categories: Action Movies, Blowing Stuff Up, and Diplomatic Immunity

Hard Drivin'

Now here's a road system you actually have to break the speed limit to get through.

9th Mar by EdwinLecter   Comments (8913)   View in Bahoogle Earth
Categories: Burning Rubber

Spot The Deliberate Mistake

We'll let you work out what's happened here. We have our own theories.

9th Mar by Flipper   Comments (20)   View in Bahoogle Earth
Categories: Weird, Inattention, and Biros

Make up to $100,000 per day just pissing around in your bedroom!

What if <u>we</u> told <u>you</u> that you could <u>quit your job</u>, noodle around with some bits of old wire all day, and <u>earn more money</u> than you ever dreamed of? And <u>then some</u>

What if <u>I</u> told <u>you</u> that <u>you</u> could work as little as 10 - 15 minutes a day? Do you think it's possible that someone with **no particularly special skills** can make $250 a minute just by typing short rhymes on a computer or the underside of a club flyer?

The answer is ABSOLUTELY POSITIVELY <u>**YES**</u>.

AND IT'S AS EASY AS A 1, 2 ...a 1, 2, 3, 4!

Just become a musician!

People just like you and me are picking up guitars, using expensive pirated studio software, writing songs and reaping the rewards of being a MUSICIAN.

- <u>**no**</u> deadlines
- <u>**no**</u> experience necessary
- <u>**not**</u> much talent needed, really, to be honest
- <u>**flexible**</u> hours, minutes
- <u>**unlimited**</u> potential earnings
- <u>**sex**</u> by the <u>**trough full**</u>

Believe me. I'm a MUSICIAN and I've got so much money I don't know what the fuck do with it. Just look at my earnings from this month alone!"

DAILY SALES SUBTOTALS:

```
Sun Sep 30  $1,198.73
Sat Sep 29    $997.13
Fri Sep 28  $1,234.56
Thu Sep 27  $7,891.01
Wed Sep 26  $1,561.91
Tue Sep 25    $753.20
Mon Sep 24  $1,772.16
Sun Sep 23  $1,262.60
Sat Sep 22  $     1.99
Fri Sep 21    $ 554.99
Thu Sep 20  $9,999.99
Wed Sep 19  $1,234.23
Tue Sep 18  $3,333.33
```

OK how does it work?

Anyone can do it! Can you come up with some weak, self-absorbed poetry? Do you have fleeting suicidal tendencies, which alternate with an inflated notion of your own talent? Of course you do.

You can be a SELF EMPLOYED MUSICIAN wherever you like, whenever you like. People will be impressed by you. You will sing songs, and they will applaud.

No stuffing envelopes! No cold calling! Just a bit of strumming and peering through your fringe! You'll love it! It's great! It's a piece of piss!

Where do I sign up?

Take the next exciting step. Your new exciting life is just one click away!

For a limited time only we have the following information packs available, depending on what kind of MUSICIAN you want to be:

- sullen, guitar-obsessed muso
- emotionally overwrought singer songwriter
- success-hungry post-stage-school muppet
- hermit-like artistic perfectionist

only **$49.99**

CLICK BELOW TO ORDER!

What we want to eat depends on how we feel.
So we've created selection of new and exciting dishes for when life takes an unfortunate turn...

All Night Garage
No need to draw straws for a 'munchies run' or to take half-an-hour shouting your order through plate glass at a sleepy cashier who'll just get in wrong anyway.

ingredients: cheap noodles, 2 Scotch Eggs, 1 bottle of chocolate milk, and 2 packets of Spring Onion flavour crisps.

Liquid Lunch
The perfect nutritionally balanced lunch for sackings and Web 2.0 startup disasters.

ingredients: 6 pints of strong lager, 2 whiskey chasers and - why not eh? - a bottle of liquer, all dusted with dry roasted peanuts, and cigarette ash.

Dumped!
They left you so why not let yourself go too? Eat like a bitter singleton. A deliciously oily kebab, dotted with an illiterate teenager's fingerprints. Flaccid, Almost-Liquid(tm) chips and a mini bottle of whiskey to momentarily wash the pain away.

Comfort Binge
Pop in the microwave and six minutes later - voila! Starch, chocolate and glucose make great sedatives and also work to temporarily fill that huge hollow in the centre of your life.

Ingredients: chocolate cake, huge slab of milk chocolate, creamy ice-cream (with chunky custard cream biscuits) and a minature bottle of port left over from christmas.

SPECIAL OFFERS
at onlineshoppingshop.com

Hello's
SUGAR
The Original & Best Breakfast

only $9.99 per lb

poudre
Powdered Mineral Water
Just Add Water!

$11.99 a bottle

Cajun
Fried Lettuce
Nutrient-stripping recipe
Mmm!
May contain traces of lettuce

only $9.99 per lb

POPCORN
TOFU

just $0.25 a kilo

'SENSATIONAL' CRISPS
VEAL FLAVOURED

new crisp flavours
Gazpacho
Fish Fingers & Curry Sauce
Potato
Diet Cola
$1.99 per pack

Spend the difference

Don't buy the slop we dollop into tins for the proles. Show you have taste by investing in this over-packaged stuff instead.

the entire range
- wrapped by the hands of newborn babies
- seasoned with salt collected from the eyes of Saharan nomads
- packaged in biodegradeable, non-wood pulp, potato starch compostable trays
- flown in on a private Lear Jet and vaccum-sealed in - oh I dunno - gold leaf?
- inspected personally by The Queen

our vegetables
- watered with the tears of the soldier children of Sierra Leone
- fertilised with Giant Panda dung

our meat
- hand reared with full quality of life (open fields, ikea chairs, 24 channel digital TV with Tivo)
- sacrificed by single lethal injection, after a special low-gravity laser ceremony a bit like that one in Logan's Run

*eat the food * buy into the lifestyle * ssssshhh everything's ok*

Posh Meats The highest quality sausage shaved from the loins of the famed Fighting Caspian Bulls plus the brains of that pig sliced to an almost transparent .08 microns

All-Butter Organic Carrot Selection An exquisitely tended carrot, gently but firmly pulled on Shrove Tuesday from the richest volcanic soil, cleaned down with squirrel tail brushes, and enhanced with lipstick and placed inside an individual glass slipcase especially for you.

Notice the difference

For the budget conscious buyer, a range of more desirable foodstuffs that combine several products in one affordable solution.

▶122

Hammy Dodgers

Cow lips & scrota
m'm's
MECHANICALLY RECOVERED
Chocolate-coated mechnically-recovered meat drops

I Can Believe It's Not *Butter!*
Margerine spray

How do you know when you're at a *Spend The Difference* dinner party?

- Do all of the girls' names end with a vowel?
- Is there more Balsamic vinegar than strictly necessary?
- Are you mildly unnerved at the sight of a switched off television?
- Are you the only person there whose education wasn't paid for?
- Does your dinner consist of a very small piece of meat "accompanied" by some orange stuff and some green stuff? Is your pudding a column towering half a foot out of your bowl and heavily laced with icing sugar? Has the icing sugar been arranged?
- Are you drinking three times as much as anyone else?
- Do you suffer a flash of blind panic when it momentarily appears that you have taken too much salad?
- When some horsey twat eventually feigns interest in your moribund existence, do you sum up your lifetime's achievement in an 8-second soundbite?
- Are you interrogated with appalled fascination by a lisping buffoon purely because you are one of several hundred thousand people to have attended a football match in your life?
- Do you grossly misunderstand the situation when someone asks you if you ride?
- Has someone mentioned that India is amazing?
- Has someone pronounced Nicaragua with a silent 'g'?
- Is some tedious hooray still banging on about his goddamn share prices?
- After 'pudding' does the resident loud-mouth tap the side of his hooter and say "Who's up for dessert?".
- Is there a tangible shudder of disgust when you announce that you're going for a burst?
- Could you care less if you never, ever saw these dead-eyed reptiles again?

amasszone.com   Your Amasszone.com | Crap Books | See All 976898 Product Categories   Your Debt | 🛒 Pile | Your Wants ⊡ ⊡ | Help!|

| Self Indulgent | Churned Out | Toilet | The New York Chronicle's ® Worst Sellers | Just Plain Unoriginal | Ghoulishly Narcissistic | Unfunny | Dead | Buried |

Notes From A Superhighway: Bill Bison Explores The Internet

by Bill Bison   Eccentric characters and entertaining anecdotes abound as Bill takes us on a whirlwind journey *inside* of the internet. Lucky he brought his notebook! The paper one! (more)

Key Phrases: late afternoon slot on BBC Radio 4, beard in USB socket, More YouTube, Vicar?, adult verification hilarity (more...)

★★★★☆ (141 customer reviews)

List Price: ~~$14.00~~
          Price: $00.20 & eligible for **FREE shipping** on orders over $25

Best Value Buy **Notes from A Superhighway** and get **O'Really's Advanced Occasional Forays Into The Outside World** at an additional 95% off Amasszone.com's everyday low price.

Quantity: 1 ▾

( ) **Add to Shopping Cart**

or

Impulsively buy now and regret later

Customers who bought this item also bought

Them Quirky Brits (US edition) by Bill Bison

Those Crazy Yanks (UK edition) by Bill Bison

Editorial Reviews

Amasszone.com review: Bill Bison has scouted the hickiest of Midwest burgs, hiked the bear-and-Dr. Pepper-infested wilderness of the Appalachian Trail and has braved the beer monsters and shrimp roasters of Australia. Gee, he's even been to England! But in "Notes from a Superhighway: Bill Bison Explores The Internet", the inoffensively irreverent travel journalist boldly goes where no writer has gone before. And this time it's digital. From the cockeyed yahoos who inhabit the town of Yahoo to the cleverer-than-thou brainiacs who make Wikipedia their home, it's a laugh-out-loud adventure of reassuringly patronising observations upon a culture that's often more zeros than ones. And just you wait until Bill discovers blogging...

"Funny" - Timed Out
"Astoundingly funny" - NewAge Scientist
"Howlingly funny" - The Unindependent
"So funny it will make your spleen burst and bile come out of your nose onto your roast dinner like gravy from the backside of an incontinent horse" - Charlie Brookner, The Preserver

See all Editorial Reviews

Inside This Book (learn more)

First Paragraph:

Things had not started well. I'd clicked my mouse three times, just as the manual advised. But I was beginning to get the uneasy sensation that we were not in Kansas any more. Instead, bags sitting indolently at my feet, I had been dumped at the port of Google, a bewilderingly brightly-lit entry terminal where deluded know-nothings swarm, mouths agog, waiting to be shunted in the right by some wayward impulse from their unconscious. Soon I was to encounter the loathsome hordes of MySpace. But that was tomorrow. Today all I needed was a bag of Krispy Kreme donuts, a credit card, and a box of Kleenex.

Customer Reviews

Average Customer Review: ☆☆☆☆☆
Write an online review and share your thoughts with other customers.

★★★★★ **Laugh? I went funny until my tummy got runny!** December 20
Reviewer: **Wendy De'Ath** - See all my reviews

Bill Bison's   books have helped me understand that not all Europeans are garlic-breathed capitulators with hairy underarms. In fact only some of them are like that; there's also the nutty Spaniards, the nasty Germans and the uproarious Swiss! But seriously, I picked this up because I'm new to the internet, having been on AOL for ten years. Yet I knew I'd be in safe hands from the word go because the usual inimitable Bison's humor and caustic side-splitting descriptions are all here.

☐ Comment | Was this review helpful to you? (Yes) (No)

☆☆☆☆☆ **Unfortunately lacking in technical accuracy**, December 23
Reviewer: **Wikipedant** - See all 68,000 of my reviews

While claiming to be a guided tour around the internet, actually Mr. Bison's   book is woefully short of precision, with numerous unforgivable errata which had me guffawing - for all the wrong reasons. In particular his tale of blocking JavaScript pop-up by using the PopBlock toolbar is clearly made up as PopBlock is Linux-native only and not Windows compatible! Plus they are based around executable server-side technologies upon which Bryson would not have been able to intrude - at least not without PHD-level understanding of procedural C++ and operator overloading techniques. So, in summary, what a total moron.

☐ Comment | Was this review helpful to you? Did it nauseate you? (Yes, us too) (No, leave my spod breathren alone)

Where's My Stuff?	**Shipping & Returns**	**Need Help?**
• Oh well finally it arrived	• Have you seen our ship?	• No goals? Click here
• And whaddya know?	• It's a big one.	• Sense of implacable unreality?
• It's the wrong order	• With our name on the side	• In shock at your ramshackle life?

| Advanced Books | Simple Books | Crap Books | The Wolverhampton Gazette ® Best Sellers | More Books | Bookos En Español | Thin Books (Magazines) | Regret Your Stuff | Ah Just Get More | Txtbks |

I Get Up: I Write This Muck
Quirky Single Guy With A Bunch Of Wry Self-Effacing Insights Into Life, Love and Living In London Threaded Into A Story About A Quirky Single Media Guy Ah You Can Do The Rest - Ole!

by Dan Blazer

⋆⋆⋆⋆⋆ (5 customer reviews)

Quantity: 1 ▾

⬤ Add to Shopping Cart

or

Sod that and buy it instantly.

List Price: ~~$27.00~~

Discount $37.80 (140%)

We pay you: $16.20 & cover your **Super Ultra Saver Shipping.** And the courier will give you oral! Details

55,696 used & new available from $0.01

Increase the information you receive in your life by signing up for Amasszone Wow!, our minute-by-minute e-mail newsletters. Discover new releases in your favorite categories, popular pre-orders and bestsellers, exclusive author interviews and podcasts, special sales, and more EVERY MINUTE! Yep that's 14440 email alerts a day.

See inside this book

See inside this book and print the pages out for free

Editorial Reviews

From Publishers Weekly Unmitigated self-indulgent claptrap. Flat, moronic cheerless navel gazing of the highest order. It should sell very well.

What do customers ultimately do after viewing this item?

88% silently bemoan the state of the book industry

6% look around the room and think "God, am I like that?"

2% visit the author's website and send him a thinly disguised offer of no-strings sex

Customer Reviews - NOW WITH HONEST FILTER(tm)

⋆⋆⋆⋆⋆ **I Am The Author Posting Under A Poorly Chosen Pseudonym**, September 19

Reviewer: **Ban Dazer** (London) - See all my reviews

"I was frankly dazzled by this book. Unique, original - a storming debut from a young punky maverick determined to rattle the world with his wryness. For all the five or six thousand naysayers who have left a review here, I have one thing to say: suck it and see. Ole!"

Comments (213) | Was this review helpful to you? (Yes) (No)

⋆⋆⋆⋆⋆ **I Am An Embittered, Less Successful Friend Of The Author** , September 19

Reviewer: **Ghandi Crug** (London) - See all my reviews

"To see this book flopped has been one of the greatest joys of my life. Who would have thought schadenfreude such an exquisite feeling? Second only to masturbating bitterly over my lack of success while Dan - whom I gave his first job, whom I read early manuscripts, whom I coached and moulded more or less in my own image, whom I lent a tenner to over three months ago and who still hasn't paid me back - while Dan's career has skyrocketed beyond my reach."

Comments (213) | Was this review helpful to you? (Yes) (No)

⋆⋆⋆⋆⋆ **I Am The Author's Ex Wife** , January 9

Reviewer: MollyBloom - See all my reviews

"This book is wonderful. Please buy it. Buy multiple copies for friends and families and enemies and strangers. By my calculation, I get at least 30p from every sale, minus lawyers fees. So buy buy buy this wonderful tome and keep me in the lifestyle I am accustomed too. And Dan, if you're reading this, return my calls, baby. You've still got my rowing machine."

Comments (213) | Was this review helpful to you? (Yes) (No)

1 of 3 people found the following review helpful:

⋆⋆⋆⋆⋆ **I Am The Author's Editor So I Guess I'd Better Wade In** , January 9

Reviewer: SecretAgentMan - See all my reviews

Hey! Well this is the single most important novel of the past century in my humble opinion. I've read a lot of trash in my time. I've even written some. This beats all of them. Hands down. I'm sending this on my Blackberry while chinning with some big jawed fucknuts in a loft restaurant! How cool is that?"

Comments (213) | Was this review helpful to you? (Yes) (No)

4 of 7 people found the following review helpful:

⋆⋆⋆⋆⋆ **I am the girl the author is writing about**, January 9

Reviewer: ABlisterInTheFun (Scottsdale, AZ USA) - See all my reviews

Look Dan this is pathetic alright. It's been 10 years since we split!!! We only went out 6 bloody months. Do you really hate me so much that you have to publish this pathetic little vendetta of a book? It's not even as if you've got the facts right. You did not break my heart by walking away across a rain swept heath as I screamed for you to come back. I chucked you after you tried to coax me into a heavy fire-lit bisexual orgy on the heath in the pouring rain. Nor did I then slide into alcoholism before ending my days in a crack den. For the record I rang you up to tell you that you were the most boring self absorbed man I'd ever met and that if you ever came near me again I'd have you beaten up. I now work as a Producer at the BBC. You, I seem to remember, were an Admin Assistant at that Estate Agents. And, for the record, you never caught me in bed with two of my closest female friends who were both hungry for cock   - though God knows you talked about the idea often enough.

Comments (213) | Was this review helpful to you? (Yes) (No)

Where's My Stuff?	Shipping & Returns	Need Help?
• Look this isn't funny anymore .	• Want to return an item?	• Forgot about the iron? Click here.
• Do you really want me to come down there with my shotgun?	• What? You don't want to keep what you bought?	• Forgot those fish fingers under the grill too?
• Because I'm going to.	• Ermmmmmmm. Get a manager someone!	• Hmmmm, yeah, wondered what that smell was

National Hypochondriacs Service

The Best Drugs

Don't let your doc fob you off with coproxamol when there are far stronger and more addictive painkillers out there

healthy living

| ASK FOR THESE THEY'RE GOOD | ARE THESE BUBOES? YES | WHEN CHOCOLATE KILLS | UNIMPRESS YOUR DOCTOR |

All the health scare information you could possibly want in one website. Whatever you think you've got, we'll make it worse.

Get up-to-the-minute alerts on plagues
Turn passing ailments into hospitalisations
Download your free stool diary & colour match chart

frequently asked questions
answered by our temps

Does my hangnail need surgery?
What's considered a calpol overdose?
Is a little knowledge really a dangerous thing?

A2Z **health encyclopedia**
horrifying ailments in alphabetical order

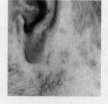

live webcam doctor
take your top off, be with you in a sec

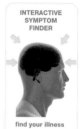

INTERACTIVE SYMPTOM FINDER

find your illness

TOP 5
New Internet Diseases

MMORPGing Sickness
Spasms of self-disgust usually felt in the abdominal area at dawn after another 24 hour binge of pointless coin gathering in the kingdom of Neverquest.

Hemorrhoids 2.0
A new bigger and brighter version of the popular anal disorder now with user-generated discontent.

Porno Claw
An affliction of the upper tarsals caused by extended periods of one handed browser shandy.

MMMyplace Peceptual Disorder
Characterised by persistent, lurid images and colours in the visual field and delusions of grandeur.

Narcissitic Neck
A chronic muscular pain caused by repeatedly posing in front of a webcam at too rakish an angle.

Latest Scare Stories

- When Organs Go Bad
  Rumbling appendix. Irritable bowel. Stroppy liver. Frothing spleen.

- Should I have sex?
  Are you crazy? Do you have any idea just how many pathogens-?

- What Would Happen To Me...?
  If I had, say, um dunno, something like the handle of a frying pan up my ass?

- Foot In Mouth?
  Ah the foot. So beautiful yet such a high potential for disfigurement and strench.

- Just Thank God You Weren't Alive Then
  Ancient agonising cures from the pre-antibiotic age.

- Doctors Barely Use The Internet
  Recent shock study shows that doctor prefer to rely on experience and training.

More Headlines

- Alcohol kills brain cells
- Study: Alcohol "good for you"
- Alcohol protects against brain injury
- Alcohol causes heart disease
- No It doesn't
- Piss off. Yes it does.

Name that rash

- ○ Scarlet Fever
- ○ Chickenpox
- ○ Scabies
- ○ Mummy!
- ○ Flee! Flee! 'Tis the pox

VOTE

View Results

Self Diagnosis
Advanced Hypochondriac Panic Syndrome | Acid House Reflux | Arse | Back | Bad Tummy | Diahorreah? | Dyeorhaeah? | Daiorreah? | The Shits | Early Onset Diagnoses | Type II Diabolism | Irritable Balls Syndrome | Men | The Pox | Stroke

The worlds of medicine and disease change and evolve at a vast and terrible rate. This site cannot be help responsible for any emerging ailments and treatments we have not been able to scare you with. See additional information.

The National Hypochrondriacs Service is wholly owned by a Bahoogle.com consortium under the government's private finance initiative

National Hypochondriacs Service

DIRTY SPONGES	GREASY HAND RAILS	BUSES	TRAIN TOILETS	INFLIGHT HEADPHONES	WARM HANDSHAKES	DIRT EVERYWHERE!

NHS Self-Diagnosis Chart

DIAGNOSIS

1. Identify primary symptoms

headache | bit hot | nothing | genital stuff | sore throat → **IT'S SARS**

2. Identify secondary symptoms

crying | phoning friend | none | squirming | vomiting → **IT'S EBOLA**

3. Diagnosis in detail

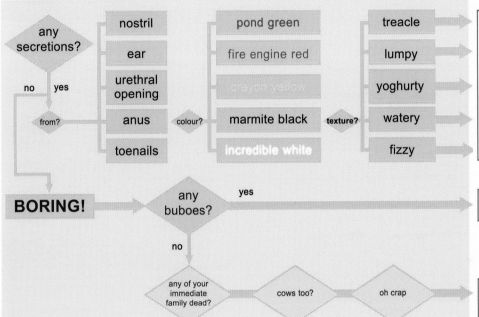

any secretions?
- no
- yes

from?
- nostril
- ear
- urethral opening
- anus
- toenails

colour?
- pond green
- fire engine red
- crayon yellow
- marmite black
- incredible white

texture?
- treacle
- lumpy
- yoghurty
- watery
- fizzy

→ **UM SORRY JUST BEING NOSEY**

BORING!

any buboes?
- yes → **IT'S BUBONIC PLAGUE**
- no

any of your immediate family dead? → **cows too?** → **oh crap** → **IT'S THE ANDROMEDA STRAIN**

DANGER SIGNS
Phone your doctor immediately if you have any of the following:

- Nurse's outfit
- Drowsiness
- Irritability
- Prurient interest in other people's ailments
- Watch ER too much
- One of those blood pressure armbands

ACTION
PANIC

hamstrjobs.com
straining to get somewhere in life, anywhere, uhhhhhh nowhere

Looking for a good job? **Hahahaha**   Looking for fresh blood?

Employers Site

My Hamstr | Find Job | Enter Wheel | Spin Round And Round | Await Happiness

Get a hamstr job
Turn the commute into a hoot!

I work for the man
And Hamstr works for him too
view stories

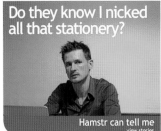
Do they know I nicked all that stationery?
Hamstr can tell me
view stories

We got the arms deal!
Hamstr cheers for me
view stories

So? Who's go is it next?
Satan's black teats wait for me
view stories

Hamstr Poll

What percentage of your workday do you spend vacantly staring into your screen as meaningless hour melts into meaningless hour?

- ○ 100%
- ○ 75%
- ○ 50%
- ○ 25%
- ○ none %

[Results]

Job Search

Enter keywords (e.g. sell out, corporate shill, sighing, staring out of the window)

Select Location
- city
- town
- industrial park
- at home in pyjamas
- the docks

Select Level
- minion
- spear carrier
- henchman (big blonde one)
- henchman (girl)
- middle management
- upper middle management
- just under the glass ceiling, licking it

Choose Your Commute
- hellish
- hungover
- caffeinated
- black sheen of dirt under everything
- sweaty handrails
- slick yellow juice
- in the fold between finger and thumb

LET'S SEE SHALL WE?

Job Hunt by sector

Check out our pointers with searches by industry:

Old Fashioned Jobs
Money & Guilt Jobs
Smug Jobs
Jobs Your Parents Won't Get
Jobs You Won't Get
Steaming Jobs

Resume Rescue

Let our bitchy experts tear into your CV. ▶ 057

Latest Crap Jobs

Call Centre Operative
Jobs entails working at a call centre to which an Indian call centre has recently outsourced its calls. **Location**: Darfur. **Starts**: Now!

Workforce Reduction Strategist
As part of our Abject Penury Devision, following a standard re-sizing of our downsizing protocols, you will be responsible for implementing our company-wide cross-site revisioning to meet growth targets ahead of our annual performance review and an audit by the tax authorities. In other words, working with the work force you will be required to get rid of them ASAP. **Starts**: Christmas Eve.

Sanitation And Waste Removal Operative
Leading metropolitan borough council requires enthusiastic blue collar workers to co-ordinate phone booth sanitisation, removal of hygiene blocks in public urinals (by hand), collecting and cleaning of needles from municipal heroin clinics, bed washing tramps, de-lousing prostitutes, slopping out public conveniences with industrial spatulas. Additionally, you will provide Health & Safety cover at large dark polysexual orgies on council parkland, and to get rid of the whomming cable some blighter has laid in my en-suite.

Dedicated Procrastination Associate
Multinational seeks listless, lackadaisical clockwatchers with substantial (3-5 year) procrastination experience. Committed pen pushing and water-cooler anecdote relay required. Roles include: re-organising bookmarks and MineMineMyPlace Buddies; adding new wistful selections to Amasszone wishlist and DVD rental queue. Your key role in the team will be to source at least one funny / outrageous / scatological YouFlue clip for others to gather around and guffaw at.

Spam Copywriter
Ci@gr@, V1AL13 , Via_grra, Cia_aliss. Can you come up with more like this? Are you at the height of your creative writing career? Two Moscow-based basement spam barons are looking for a wordsmith to come up with ever more creative ways to circumvent anti-spam technology. Contact: Baron P. Woostla-ser or Barthomelow F. Disgust. Note:we will not pass your email onto any one else).

---

hamstrjobs.com has emailed its cv to HR at Bahoogle.com. They are currently reviewing it and will get be in touch if it's suitable (i.e. it's being shredded for hamster nests)

hamstrjobs.com
straining to get a job somewhere, anywhere, uhhhh nowhere

Looking for a job? Log in   Looking to hire?

Employer site →

Post jobs | Search resumes

Get off the wheel| For Two Weeks | Come back | Get Back On It

Resume Rescue
Not sure if your CV is hard-working enough? Watch and learn as our employment experts tighten this top resume's ass.

Katherine Merchant - Curriculum Vitae
chief executive officer with pan-global experience

> Katherine omits a picture of herself. FATAL MISTAKE! How will she be taken seriously in the boardroom without one? Silly girl.

PERSONAL QUALITIES

- one of the boys, can take my drink and just unattractive enough to not be a distraction
- deep psychological wounds even my weekly Reiki group can't ease
- heavily drugged but alert
- childless (but thinking of asking a gay friend to inseminate me)
- huge mortgage, large car, several large but needy dogs
- hard worker, often in the office till gone 9pm, whereupon I go home and tranquillise myself with triviality (television mostly, or a valium if I can find one)

EXPERIENCE

CEO, ComComDotCom.Com, Oct 2005 - present
Responsible for web publishing and e-marketing of over 135 websites to over 1000 countries. Manage a team of hopeless muttons whom I shift idly around the world like chess pieces. That takes a small portion of the day. In between lunch and dinner and shopping research trips, I manage a comprehensive online dating profile which provides distraction and false hope for loving companionship 24/7.

Managing Director, MoreGettingAndCommuneOkayShone.com, July 2004 - Aug 2005
Started my own e-marketing business in a Prozac-assisted flash of inspiration. The company offered a range of services to small and medium-sized companies which we just copied and pasted from a central document and then changed the company name on the top of the PowerPoint document.
- Learnt not to elevate friends and family, especially not your mother, into key financial positions.
- Managed clients: listened to their crappy ideas before doing the opposite, nursing their insecurities, taking them out for a drink, bit of flirty banter, yes that's my thigh but let's sign the deal first shall we?
- Directed all core marketing activties such as posting things, phoning people up, browsing the Net, emailing, chatting.

PR Director, DropDeadLoans, Aug 2003-July 2004
Sold meaningless commodities to anxious consumers.
- Managed PR launches, PR lunches, PR hunches,
- Developed a bit of a PR paunch but later worked that off via an eating disorder
- Suffered from bad dreams and used drugs to sleep
- Mastered my mwahh! air kiss
- Realised that appearance is more important that what you say.

> Poor layout here results in an unsightly gap. Plus there's no mention of exactly which drugs she took to sleep. Remember: it's all in the details!

> Katherine could go into more detail here

Sabbatical due to nervous breakdown, 2001-2004

Joint-Founder, Internet Life Coaching, Flower Delivery and Takeaway Pizza dotcom startup, 1999-2001
- co-ordinated a diverse network of national website managers while not understanding a single word I was saying
- managed budget for trendy office decor (Grifters, pool table, free pastries, 42-inch plasma screens, Star Trek captain's chair with working phaser buttons etc)
- wrote, rewrote, and finally ditched business plan for an ad-hoc day-by-day 'this'll come out in the wash' business structure
- planned our enforced relocation from central London to Feltham
- took on responsibility as our team shrunk, managing human resources, customer support, marketing, strategic development and the canteen

Fashion PR Director, 1997-2001
Lorded it over pretty young assistants. Became frustrated at the high homosexual male count of the industry. Went to parties. Took cocaine, ecstasy and vodka, sometimes in enema form. Managed to steal over 600 separate items of clothes.

Fashion PR assistant, 1994-1997
Was lorded over by ball-busting bitch boss. Responsibilities included: flirting with photographers and sometimes sleeping with them. Managed to steal just 200 items, but was happy with this as I made some good friends.

Qualified Interim Marketing Communications Adjunct, 1991-1994
No idea what my job was supposed to be, or what I was supposed to do, but it didn't matter. I was having fun. Made coffee, played solitaire, shuffled paper, browsed hard, pretended to work and just chatted instead. Became the champion of Mind Sweeper in the office. Felt part of a team. Made loads of great friends. Everything felt like an adventure. It was great.

> Katherine is talking too much about how she feels as a human being which is always a big no-no for employers who are interested in HARD FACTS intermixed with MADE UP STUFF

 **Bullies Reunion**
millions of old victims listed

DinnerLadies Reunion
you want chips with that?

Cliques Reunion
want to join? well you can't

Abductees Reunion
swap anal probe stories

 **Bullies Reunion**

What are your old victims doing now?

Bullies Reunion is a site for those of us who spent our schooldays tormenting, ridiculing and psychologically disturbing other children who were smaller, weirder, younger, poorer - or, indeed, richer than ourselves. Kids who wore glasses. Kids who walked a bit funny. Kids who needed go to the toilet too often. You can find old victims you've lost touch with, discover how much they're earning now and get back in touch and organise massive bundles.

1 Which old victims do you want to find?

Most members choose their primary school mates first, but you can also track back to the building sites where you played all day while your mum worked the streets.

2 See which names you remember

Southend High Class of 1993
Christine Yikes
Sarah Yomyom
Gladys Yachtliver
Peter Zorrgoroth, Son of Zorgoran

We'll show you a list of victims who were at the same place as you, at the same time. You'll be surprised how many names you remember.

3 Discover what they're up to now

 Left for the big city to make my fortune. And I did mostly by stealing from friends. Most nights I masturbate to get to sleep. Life is schweet!

It's fascinating being nosy and reading how people's lives turned out! Plus, if you feel like beating them up again, send them a message safely through the site.

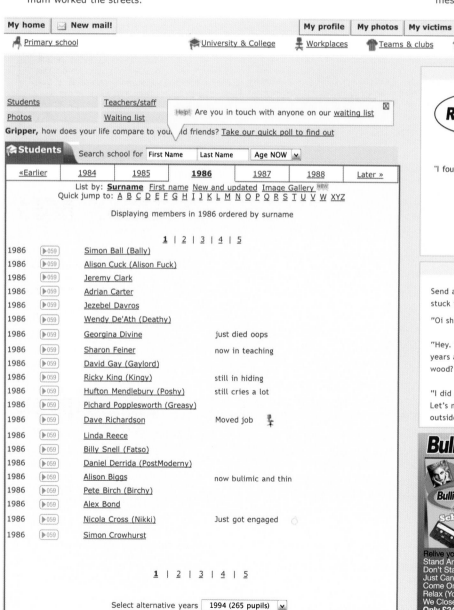

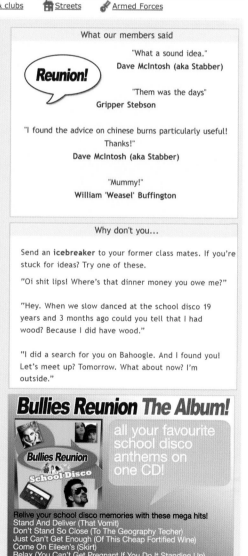

| My home | ✉ New mail! | | My profile | My photos | My victims | My weapons | My feeble bullies' | Heart |

🏠 Primary school   🎓 University & College   🏃 Workplaces   🏟 Teams & clubs   🏠 Streets   🎸 Armed Forces

Students   Teachers/staff
Photos   Waiting list

Help! Are you in touch with anyone on our waiting list ⊠

Gripper, how does your life compare to you old friends? Take our quick poll to find out

🎓 **Students**   Search school for [First Name] [Last Name] [Age NOW ▾]

| «Earlier | 1984 | 1985 | **1986** | 1987 | 1988 | Later » |

List by: **Surname**   First name   New and updated   Image Gallery NEW
Quick jump to: A B C D E F G H I J K L M N O P Q R S T U V W XYZ

Displaying members in 1986 ordered by surname

1 | 2 | 3 | 4 | 5

1986	▶059	Simon Ball (Bally)	
1986	▶059	Alison Cuck (Alison Fuck)	
1986	▶059	Jeremy Clark	
1986	▶059	Adrian Carter	
1986	▶059	Jezebel Davros	
1986	▶059	Wendy De'Ath (Deathy)	
1986	▶059	Georgina Divine	just died oops
1986	▶059	Sharon Feiner	now in teaching
1986	▶059	David Gay (Gaylord)	
1986	▶059	Ricky King (Kingy)	still in hiding
1986	▶059	Hufton Mendlebury (Poshy)	still cries a lot
1986	▶059	Pichard Popplesworth (Greasy)	
1986	▶059	Dave Richardson	Moved job
1986	▶059	Linda Reece	
1986	▶059	Billy Snell (Fatso)	
1986	▶059	Daniel Derrida (PostModerny)	
1986	▶059	Alison Biggs	now bulimic and thin
1986	▶059	Pete Birch (Birchy)	
1986	▶059	Alex Bond	
1986	▶059	Nicola Cross (Nikki)	Just got engaged
1986	▶059	Simon Crowhurst	

1 | 2 | 3 | 4 | 5

Select alternative years [1994 (265 pupils) ▾]

What our members said

"What a sound idea."
Dave McIntosh (aka Stabber)

Reunion!

"Them was the days"
Gripper Stebson

"I found the advice on chinese burns particularly useful! Thanks!"
Dave McIntosh (aka Stabber)

"Mummy!"
William 'Weasel' Buffington

Why don't you...

Send an **icebreaker** to your former class mates. If you're stuck for ideas? Try one of these.

"Oi shit lips! Where's that dinner money you owe me?"

"Hey. When we slow danced at the school disco 19 years and 3 months ago could you tell that I had wood? Because I did have wood."

"I did a search for you on Bahoogle. And I found you! Let's meet up? Tomorrow. What about now? I'm outside."

Bullies Reunion
they're still here!

Reunion Reunion
were you on here in 99? I was

Busstops Reunion
Were you waiting for the 35 too?

Bullies Reunion

Simon Ball (Bally)

What Simon is doing

After Uni, entered the world of corporate finance. My days are now an endless succession of memos, chits, ledgers and spreadsheets. My evenings are a ceaseless tedium of microwaved meals and sighing. For enjoyment I like to look at my car. When and how will it all end? If anyone knows, please email me.

Alison Cuck

What Alison is doing

Since leaving school I have been mostly indoors. I live in London with my dog, Bisto. In 1998 I began to slowly merge with my filthy sofabed, and two years later we decided to get married. Now, my body is a mass of weeping sores, and my mind is composed entirely of celebrity gossip and daytime television. Hey I may not have achieved much, but at least I can eat ketchup sandwiches all day

Jeremy Clark

What Jeremy is doing

Since leaving school - my career has grown from strength to strength. However I am trying to get hold of Mark 'the Hammer' Davis who used to be a 4th year at my school.
Mark, I'm still saving my dinner money for you - which currently stands at £16,940. Please mail me and I'll be happy to pay up . I've already scuffed my shoes for you and ripped my tanktop - so should save you time on collection.

Adrian Carter (Get Carter)

What Adrian is doing

Not married. No kids. I'm impotent, actually. Never told anyone that before. Don't know why I said it here. Got to get these things off your chest, I guess.

Jezebel Davros

What Jezebel is doing

Wanted to be a doctor and help people, but got into IT and the Web instead, was a project manager for a major dotcom startup that collapsed, worked the docks for a time, then got involved in a radicla Web 2.0 start up, that folded, now I am back at my spot down the docks, wanking for coins.

Wendy De'Ath (Deathy)

What Deathy is doing

I started my own business earlier this year. The business is called Four Seasons Candle Co. I am selling hand-poured scented candles and accessories. If you love candles then you will love my candles. They have a strong scent throw. Thanks Deathy.

Sharon Feiner

What Sharon is doing

Left school, worked as a supervisor in the local Woolworths for 10 years, married, two kids, Lee (5) and Liza (2), divorced, still go to the local in the hope of seeing some of you. Everyone seems to have left town. Email me. Please.

David Gay (Gaylord)

What Gaylord is doing

I am currently in prison. It wasn't me.

Rick King (Kingy)

What Rick is doing

Hey, everyone! I'm a member of a cool new church called the love Of God Community Church! It's just opposite Argos on the High Street! Come along! You might be surprised! It's not at all how you would expect! Seriously!

Hufton Mendlebury (Poshy)

What Poshy is doing

I graduated from Manchester University in 1989, and fell into a period of sustained heroin abuse. I am currently working as a crackwhore at Junction 26 of the M1. Come by. I do mates rates.

Richard Popplesworth (Greasy)

What Greasy is doing

You may remember me as the greasy kid at school with the VIC-20. Well! I graduated from Birmingham Uni and have been working as a consultant ever since. I now drive a bright yellow TVR. I mix with "friends" with good teeth called Hugo and drink in Broadgate circle. And Billy Anderson, I saw you on Islington High St the other day laughing with your wife, HA!..I was in a TVR and was sporting Paul Smith cuff links....you were not!

Billy McLoud (Fatso)

What Fatso is doing

After having an enormous lottery win 14 months ago, I am now living the Life Of Riley. Using my enormous manor house as a base, I spend all my time travelling around the world with my gorgeous model fiancee Candice, and we are currently looking at purchasing most of Andorra to use as our sexual playground for six months of the year. Life is fantastic, rammed with drugs, drink, wealth, splendour and sex - and every day I wake up and thank God for gambling.

Parentingsureisfun.com

What Type Of Parent Are You?

Grumpy old Davros from CynicalDad posted this. We don't normally tune into his stuff (too dark!) but we made an exception as this was funn-ee.

The Micro-managers No Timmy don't do that. Push it that way. Move it over here. Come here. No! Do it this way. Uhhhh get out the way! I'll do it you incompetent brat.

Soppy mumsie wumsie doo dah My Timmy is tri-lingual. My Timmy built an entire hacienda with his bricks. My Timmy shits gold. If you reflexively slip into an endless stream of anecdotes about your offspring in lieu of real conversation, this is you.

The Why Did We Do This To Ourselves? Middle class narcissists just basically in shock that one romantic dream and a bit of careless 'rhythm method' later and their hedonistic, self-obsessed lives are basically finito.

The Left It Too Lates But don't worry we'll get a couple of dinosaur-sized dogs instead.

The Paranoids Never leave the house without your baby wipes, sterilising kit, anti-bacterial handwash, and defibrillator.

The Wolf Family You were brought up too strictly as a child so you've vowed to do the opposite with your offspring. The *exact opposite*. No boundaries. No rules. Just feral monster kids who crap all up the stairs.

Got any more?

[posted by QueenMummy 4.30 am | 12 comments | 3 spam comments]

5 New Ways To Give Birth

Some exciting new birthing trends from America. Say "meh" to the birthing pool and mymy to these babies...

- bungee birthing it just pops out apparently
- low gravity messy but wonderfully free
- caramel birthing pool what could be softer?
- birthing with dolphins fully-trained female ones
- Oprah Winmpole as your birth partner expensive but totally ultimate

[posted by QueenMummy 3.03 am | 12 comments | 3 adverts for replica watches]

Mucrosoft Parent

Mucrosoft
ToughParent

Mucrosoft

No matter what kind of parent you are - old school, new wet, hands off or just plain 'abusive' - this new software package will help. Co-ordinates with all your wireless appliances so you can control punishments and the 'naughty step' from your sofa. Reads stories to your kid. Gets their clothes ready in the morning. Ah gawd why doesn't this really exist?

[posted by QueenMummy 6.43 am | 49 comments | 7 offers of easy university diplomas]

Celebrity Parenting Tips

Author Mary Snyder has interviewed bevvy of celebrity mums and brought you this, a range of everyday tips for maximum motherhood.

```
• When you're tired, get nanny to take baby for 4 hours while you
get some sleep
• If your child has a tantrum, give her to nanny and go upstairs and
have a brief cry.
• If baby isn't sleeping very well, get nanny to sit up with him.
• If you get depressed, try buying a new car or a new villa in a
beautiful location.
```

[posted by QueenMummy 5.12 am | 980 comments | 957 abusive]

★ **Cute Gallery**
Your latest pictures

 I love the smell of meconium in the morning

Oh hahah he puked all over me.

Cute! He tried to gouge my eye out!

 ★ **Party Themes**
Download invites, wrapping paper for every birthday.

chaos

VOMITY

EXTRA VOMITY

★ **In The Forums**
• Sleeping through Help!
• My Timmy's slept through from 6 weeks!
• My Esmerelda has slept through since she was born!
• Pah! My Phillipe hasn't woken up for 3 years.

★ **About**
Hi there. We're Tim and Linda. We have around 14 beautiful children and a lovely big house. We're friendly, outgoing, spoontaneous, rich and still in touch with our inner children. Linda's never been depressed and neither has Tim! We don't get asthma. Our car never breaks down. Everything's sorted! This is our blog exploring our dedicated and full lives as parents.

★ **Categories**

Noise (73)
Mess (112)
Turmoil (97)
Peace (0)
Quiet (6)
Desperation (18)
Wine (190)
Sleep (0)
Regret (16)
Love (25)
When They're Asleep (4)

Parentingsureisfun.com

BabyBlog
We asked a some hi-tech friends if their newborn would like to keep a blog? They said yes!

18th August
A very exciting day! I got to meet Mummy and Daddy for the very first time. They were absolutely enormous - much bigger than me! They were quite surprised, as apparently I arrived a teensy bit early, which put mummy is a spin because she had everything planned - including her birth partner. But she couldn't make it - and daddy was away - so daddy's dad, Martin, who was down to have his waterworks looked at, had to step in. That wasn't ideal, at all. But apparently "the morphine helped".
[posted by QueenMummy 6.43 am | 12 comments]

19th August
Well, they're over the shock now and they spent quite a lot of time looking and me and making funny noises. It's quite strange not to be inside Mummy any more, but I suppose I'll get used to it. Oh, it's all very exciting, but we're all tired, and grumpy, especially dad. Martin is still hanging around. He seems to have bonded with mummy. Anyway more tomorrow.
[posted by QueenMummy 4.23 am | 12 comments]

20th August
Hmm. Mummy and Daddy took me home today. Not what I was expecting - a rather tasteless terraced house on the outskirts of suburbia. They have an irritating dog called Sam - it's daddy's dog apparently from a previous relationship - that keeps invading my space in a rather aggressive fashion. I've been propped up for most of the day in this padded seat with precious little to keep me occupied. I showed my distaste for the breast milk diet by throwing up violently over Mummy's Belle Nora slippers.
[posted by QueenMummy 3.10 am | 12 comments]

21st August
Everyone's still asleep so I get to write my own entry. Aaaaaaaaoooooowtwwjw[i 0 e[eofowe[fop'wfe\mc cq a aaaaa aa jepwepwaa
[posted by QueenMummy 5.59 am | 12 comments]

22nd August
My father is doing my head in. He's cooing over me like I'm some kind of imbecile. I got him back by screaming like a bastard for most of last night, so he's knackered, which is great, but so am I, which isn't.
[posted by QueenMummy 3.33 am | 12 comments]

23rd August
What a great day! I've been sleeping on Mummy's chest, and I've had lots of visitors, who all brought lovely presents for me, including a rattle, a cuddly dog and a plastic ball that bounces up and down, and lots of cheap plastic nonsense from Argos that's going straight in the bin! Mummy and Daddy got a bottle of champagne! Which they polished off pretty quickly. They're talking quite heatedly now.
[posted by QueenMummy 4.50 am | 12 comments]

5th May
Sorry there haven't been any entries for six months. Not much has changed except Mummy and I have a drink at the same time now. It's nice. I drink out of her lovely cuddly breast and she drinks out of a big green glass bottle. Then mummy and I like to have sleepy time together.
[posted by QueenMummy 3.00 am | 12 comments]

6th May
Daddy's still trying to get me interested in the new computer he bought for everyone. We sit there for hours in the morning showing me colourful windows and moving stuff that looks quite boring. I keep trying to see who all mummies I can see poking out from behind the windows, but he doesn't let me. They seem quite happy, whatever they're doing.
[posted by QueenMummy 4.45 am | 12 comments]

11th May
Daddy still seems to be angry that I puked up all inside his computer. Apparently he lost of lot of his important picture and videos. Mummy seemed confused by this as Daddy is an accountant. But Daddy refused to go into detail.
[posted by QueenMummy 6.01 am | 12 comments]

15th May
Dad has taken to smoking funny-smelling cigarettes out of the window. He seems to be much friendlier when he comes back though. Mummy seems unhappy at this. My daddy is a big thinker. It's one of his favourite things to do. When he goes out the front door mummy says "where are you going?" Daddy says: "Out. I need to think."
[posted by QueenMummy 6.52 am | 12 comments]

18th August
Mummy and I invented this really good game which we play all day every day. I start crying then she copies me. I cry louder and she copies me. After a while she stops which is good because it means I win. I don't know where daddy has gone. I haven't seen him for weeks.
[posted by QueenMummy 8.10am | 12 comments]

Home · You · Organize · Contacts · Groups · Explorer · [Search your photos] Search

Board Games 8 photos / 0 views

Sets | Tags | Archives | Favorites | Popular | Profile

These are some of the rare and collectible board games I've found in second hand shops and on Kakbuy. I hope you enjoy them. If you like one, make me an offer! Visit my website. ▶140

House Trap

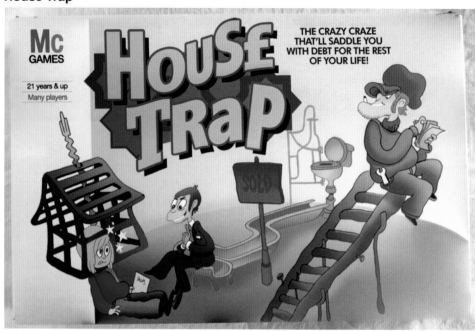

"I bought this on Kakbay. Bloody expensive!!! I had to outbid about twenty people. When I got it, It seemed to have all the part but none of the bits seem to work as described. WTF? 5 comments

Only friends, family & readers see this. Change?
0 comments

Threeway

Cocaine

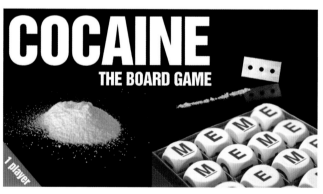

Only friends, family & readers see this. Change?
0 comments

Only friends, family & readers see this. Change?
0 comments

Board Games 2 8 photos / 0 views

Sets | Tags | Archives | Favorites | Popular | Profile

Abduction

Only friends, family & readers see this. Change?
0 comments

This looks like a lot of fun!

Only friends, family & readers see this. Change?
0 comments

I Think I've Met That Guy!

Only friends, family & readers see this. Change?
0 comments

For A Rainy Day?

Only friends, family & readers see this. Change?
0 comments

MAGICK DATING
MIDDLE WORLD'S PREMIERE PERSONALS SERVICE

KHAKHANDAR
Shropshar
Black Death
Valley Of DoomLand
ElfWorld
(amusement park)
Ye Hills

| Home | Create your free profile | Browse profiles | Subscribe | News & views | Help |

Come on in, the water's lovely

Magick Dating is a unique dating site where you can get to know a group of truly like-minded creatures and monsters, and hopefully meet that special someone. We provide a safe, secure and anonymous way to find and communicate with races of your choice.

Our members

While we are a friendly fun-loving bunch we do have a bunch of rules. By signing up to Magick Dating you agree to abide to the following:

- No spell-casting or love potions on a first date.
- No curses, rings of invisibility, or weird-ass crystal balls that let you control people at a distance.
- You must be alive to use this service. Ghosts, spectres, ghouls and wraiths are barred from this service.
- You may not publish offensive content. This includes pictures of slayings, beheadings and axe wounds.
- No spiders.

This site is a black speech free zone. We will not tolerate pluralism or tolerance in any form. Members who are racially inoffensive may be barred.

How to get started

If you want to start exchanging emails with other creatures, you'll need to become a full member by choosing one of these subscription options:

1 day: 3 groats
1 months: 1 gold coin
3 months: 2 gold coins
1000 years: 90 gold coins

Useful tips

To stop receiving messages from a member, just click on the 'slay him or 'clove her' links in their profile.

Featured profiles:

manicminer
I am Khahandar, son of Hahandir, grandson of Kahahahandir, heir to the throne of Aroth, carrier of the sixteenth seal of the mighty KhazardLords and - oh I seem to have run out of space.

bigwand
I am 7000 years old but my friends say I only look about 3000. I'm sick of selfish dwarf chicks who are all me, me, mithril so I've come here to explore other options.

goblin
Well I never thought I would end up here but then life is what you make it, right? I like: killing, gutting, slashing, stabbing and painting. But don't worry - when we meet, it'll be MORDOR.

miss_elf
No needy balrogs. No slavering wargs. No thin-lipped wizards with bushy eyebrows. Looking for cute halflings, kingly men, or dwarf princes with huge hoardes ONLY.

sophia from arabia
Hi. Welcome! I've studied Middle English sinse Autumn. It's very! I want like to meet handsome guys and guys to practice my frrench. Kisses! You gotta laugh!

BOLLOXPEDIA
The Fact-Free Encylopedia

main page

navigation
- Main Page
- Made up contents
- Featured bollox
- Current bollox
- Random Bollox

[Go] [Search]

interaction
- About Bolloxpedia
- Make a donation
- And another
- And another
- Forever
- We're Not
- Going Away

In other languages
- BASIC
- Bobspeak
- C++++++
- CB Radio
- Clickyspeak
- Coalmining
- Esperanto
- Fortran
- Frenchies
- Innuendo
- Kinaray-a
- Lipreading
- Polari
- Sexytalk
- Silbo-Gomero
- Simlish
- Sullen-teenager
- Susquehannock
- Swearing
- Tamne
- Tämne
- Temne
- Tonguetwisters
- Walloon
- Русский
- 日本語
- Norsk (bokmål)
- Српски / Srpski
- Укра⊠нська
- 中文
- Come on
- You're Just
- Making This Up

Welcome to Bolloxpedia
the free encylopedia that anyone - yes anyone! - can edit

1, 680, 974 made up articles

Today's featured article

A **cushion** (from Old French coisson, coussin; from Latin culcita, meaning 'ground scrotum'), is a soft bag of some ornamental material, usually garish and clashing with the sofa it's placed on, stuffed with wool, hair, feathers, polyester staple fiber, non-woven extremely flammable material, or even paper torn into fragments. It may be used for sitting or kneeling upon, or to soften the hardness or angularity of a chair, couch or hard ground especially during rough or spontaneous sex. They can be placed on sunloungers and used to prevent annoyances from moist grass, biting insects, brambles and broken cider bottles. If left outside, however, they quickly become sodden and rubbish.

Archive - More Featured Articles...

Did you know...

From Bolloxpedia's newest articles:

...that honey is the only food that does not spoil. Honey found in the tombs of Egyptian pharoahs has been tasted by archaeologists and found edible. The mummies however tasted dry and Tutenkahmun was found to be a "a bit chewy".

...that beetles taste like lobster, wasps like walnuts, and worms like really horrible pus-filled sausages writhing in your mouth, you goddamn bug eating low-life.

...that of all the words in the English language, 'munch' is the gayest.

...Adolf Hitler was a vegetarian and had only one testicle. The other is hidden somewhere in London's Royal Albert Hall, a premiere arts venue.

...that you can't kill yourself by holding your breath. But you can kill yourself by inserting an oily knitting needle into your eye.

...that 45% of people believe in deja vu.

...that 45% of people believe in deja vu.

...the elephant is the only mammal that can't jump. It does however have a huge dobber.

...trees used to live longer that people?

Archive - Start A New Article...

In the news

- According to the UN today, the aardvark has regained its position at the top of the alphabetical list of animals for the 532rd consecutive year.
- The world of science is rocked by an independent study that has revealed that eating a quantity of carrot may help to prevent against some cancers, maybe.
- Four men have been found in a van in Grenoble, France, making good progress en route to Rumilly, approximately 95 kilometres away along the A41/E712.
- The British Home Secretary urged restraint today in effects to calm a bloody minded SMS message war that has broken out between gangs of youths in Peckham, South London. So far, over 20 youths have been dissed and over 98 have been seriously hurt by insults.

Bolloxnews - Recent Deaths - More current events

On this day...

303 BC - Roman Emperor Sodomus woke up and did his thing.

1779 - French forces launch a failed invasion of Britain using boats and swords. Hah hah. Puny foreigners.

1946 - Prince Albert XXX becomes King Of Holland.

1971 - I was born and my favourite colour is blue.

1905 - Spamonium (element 126) is discovered by Dr Marvellous T.Lipgloss

1955 - Liverpudlian-born Turkish novelist Mehmet Targan wins the Nobel Prize for his masterpiece Bilinmeyen Heckarz Likk

1926 - Emily Earhart flies solo across the Atlantic. She becomes the last woman to make a transatlantic flight without being hit upon.

1970 - Controversial 1970's sitcom "Who's The Blackie Next Door?" ends. The long-running series stirred much protest in the press of the time for its depiction of women.

Archive - More Anniversaries....

Today's featured picture

Boy Trooper Badges Badges are a way of recognising an individual skill or for those who have taken part in an activity for a long time. Early in the 21st century the Boy Trooper Association modified and radically overhauled its range of its awards. The new selection was designed to be more in tune with moden life and "reflect the values and aspirations of 21st century youth" . The new badges stirred a great deal of controversy in the popular press.

NPOV Disputed Pages

The following pages are currently under dispute regarding their Neutral Point of View (NPOV)

Science v. Religion

Nature v Nuture

The AA vs The RAC

Blackjacks v Fruitsalads

Light Brown Toast vs Crunchier Browner Toast

Baby Throwing

God, existence of

God, colour of

God, mouthfeel of

People Inexplicably Dressed As Poodles

Who's A Pretty Boy Zen (Buddhist Self-Help Book)

Big Black Dentist's Chair

 Bolloxtionary

 Bolloxnews

 Bolloxquote

 Bolloxbooks

 Bolloxspecies

 Bolloxsource

| article | discussion | edit this page | history |

BOLLOXPEDIA
The Fact-Free Encyclopedia

navigation
- Main Page
- Made up contents
- Featured bollox
- Current bollox
- Random Bollox
- Add Bollox

search

[Go] [Search]

The pedantry **of this article is to be** applauded
Please clap on the talk page

Hassel Davidoff

From Bolloxpedia, the fact free encylopedia
(Redirected from Cognitive Neuroscience)

Hassel Davidoff is a male[1] of the homo sapiens species, a bipedal primate mammal capable of abstract reasoning and creating complex social structures, and one of currently over 6.5 billion homo sapiens currently roaming the planet Earth, the fifth largest planet of the solar system and thought to be the only body in the universe which can support life as we know it. About 70% of the surface of the planet is covered in water, forming vast water bodies such as seas and oceans, and the other 30% consists of land. The shape of the earth approximates an oblate spheroid, with variations of up to 8,850 above sea level (Mount Everest) and 10,924m below sea level (the Mariana Trench[2].) In comparison to a perfect ellipsoid, the Earth has, therefore, a tolerance of around 0.17%, which is less than the 0.22% permitted in snooker balls used in the popular cue sport played on a large baize-covered table with pockets in each of the four corners and in the middle of each of the long side cushions. Snooker balls are generally sold in groups of 22: 15 reds, black, pink, blue, brown, green, yellow and white and are made out of thermoset resin, a synthetic organic polymer which sets permanently when heated. Such balls were one of the first items produced in the development of plastics back in the mid-19th century; the popularity of billiards meant that, at the time, demand for ivory balls[3] was causing the mass slaughter of elephants for their tusks, extremely long teeth which protrude from the mouth even when closed. It is also a double-album by Anglo-American supergroup Fleetwood Mac. Released on October 19th, 1979, it failed to reach the huge level of success associated with its[4] predecessor, the multi-million selling "Rumours". The name of the album was inspired by an exhibit in a museum in the English town of Saffron Walden, a rural market town with a population of around 20,000. It was first settled in the Bronze and Iron age, but would have to wait until the Norman invasion of 1066 before further expansion, with the building of a stone church. During medieval times it thrived due to its trade in wool, but by the 17th century had become known for growing the saffron crocus which gave the town its name. The extracts from the flower, yellow in colour, were used as a dye, and also a perfume and medicine a branch of the health science that makes people feel much better, thus enabling them to achieve betterment, a term used particularly in connection with the increased value given to real property[5]. Real property is referred to as immovable property in the country of Bangladesh, a densely populated country in south east Asia, surrounded on all sides by India except for a small land border with Myanmar, and particularly prone to flooding, a situation where an area of low-lying land is covered in water, a chemical substance composed of one oxygen atom and two hydgrogen atoms of which 2^6 litres should be consumed daily by humans, including the late Pope Pius XII. He reigned throughout World War II and until October 1958, famously invoking papal infallibility in encyclical *Munificentissimus Deus*, which is Latin for the most bountiful God, the word used by monotheistic faiths to denote the creator or sustainer of the universe. Other words for God include Yahweh, Deus and Abba, which is Aramaic for daddy and also a Swedish pop group of the mid 1970s comprising Björn Ulvaeus, Benny Andersson, Agnetha Fältskog and Anni-Frid "Frida" Lyngstad. The[7] latter was a brunette, her hair characterised by higher levels of the dark pigment eumelanin and lower levels of the pale pigment phaeomelanin, which is also found abundantly in the penis, the external male sexual organ which can also be found on the lower body area of Hassel Davidoff. Olé![8]

Hassel Davidoff

Davidoff caught unawares during activity

Current Verifiable Data Readout

Date of Birth	19-14-20968
Current house number	2
TMR0IE	0Bh, 8Bh
Brake horsepower	Substantial
Legimate No Trump Bid	15-18 HCPs
Interconnect Resistance	You bet

Hassel Davidoff [edit]

Hassel Davidoff [edit]

References and notes [edit]

1. ^ Blumenstein, P.L. (1983). The Insertion of Continuous Glass Fibers within the adult male. New York: Gruber Scientific, 2-94. ISBN 0-434-41109-7.

2. ^ James Nelson considered Trench, McTrench and De La Trench to be the "only three javelin throwers of the twentieth century who had any real natural talent". Diary of An Athletics Obsessive, 21 July 1968, quoted in Diary of a Diary of An Athletics Obsessive by Richard Horabin, p. 28, Oxford University Press (1989) ISBN 0-19-282365-6

3. ^ Wei Lang, Deborah R Kelly, Rashmi Singh, James R Turvin , et al. "Well-done meat intake and billiards: The Hidden Cost." Journal of the Meat'n'Billiards Institute. Oxford: Nov 18, 1898.Vol. 90, Iss. 22; pg. 1724, 6 pgs.

4. ^ "Smith, where Jones its its 'its', its its 'its its'. 'Its its' its it's the examiner's approval." Fryslân Hasgaaaaard: 101 Anecdotes For Grammar Fascists, Wageningen DIY Bookpress, 1983.

5. ^ Stéphane Leboeuf and Hortense Gualde, "The Responsibility of History" (La responsibilité de l'histoire, in L'Histoire n°310, June 2006, pp.38 (article from pp.38 to 49, omitting pp. 41-42 which contain pictures, resuming pp.43-47, not 48, then 49)

6. ^ Monthly Mean of Occurrences of Number 2. Data: MMO Central Data Bureau. Retrieved on 2006-03-08.

7. ^ World's Most Respected The: Diverse The Vie for Attention, (Copyright: The Westmoreland Times Limited), "...the world's most respected the, as ranked by important brains from people. The top five are the, the, the, the and the.", CSR Europe, 15th December 2000

8. ^ Oh, something or other, I don't know.

External links [edit]

Hassel Davidoff ⤤ at the Internet Caucasian Human Database ⤤ [login and password required]
Hassel Davidoff's MineMineMyPlace page ⤤
Hassel Davidoff Slashfiction Fanblog ⤤ [includes graphic depictions of fictional sexual acts with people who both are and are not Hassel Davidoff]
"Why We Hate Hassel Davidoff" ⤤ – a searing indictment of Hassel Davidoff by some of his closest friends
Hassel Davidoff's Online Banking page ⤤
Hassel Davidoff And The Friendly Bear ⤤ – short novella by Hassel Davidoff aged 7
Antarctic Lingerie World: Hassel Davidoff ⤤

Categories: Births in or out of wedlock I Cameroonian nurses I Oxbow lakes I Article containing words rhyming with "sac" I Incidents on board moving boats I Nice thing I Enhancements I Lozenge I Above and beyond the call of duty I Docker I Miner I Between the wars I Imperialist Mints I Ways of saying "hello" I XPQW I In I Out I Shake it all about I Tracksuit manufacturers outside Knebworth I Padding I Trestle Tables I The Glee Council I Neither I Nor I Supposed routes from out of there I Vials I Portmanteau I Undoubtably accountable I Equinoxed I Former leaders of South Bedfordshire District Council I Wattle I Daub I Blokes my dad's mate Jeff knows I

BOLLOXPEDIA
The Fact-Free Encyclopedia

The puerility **of this article is to be** applauded
Please snigger into your lunch

navigation
- Main Page
- Made up contents
- Featured bollox
- Current bollox
- Random Bollox

navigation

- Main Page
- Made up contents
- Featured bollox
- Current bollox
- Random Bollox
- Add Bollox

search

[Go] [Search]

March 9th

From Bolloxpedia, the fact free encyclopedia

March 9th is the 54th day of the year in the Gregorian Calendar, the 9567 in the Islamic Calendar, and the 19th Day Of Great Foreboding in the Agoraphobic's Calendar.

Events

- 4000 BC - Textiles made of hemp are first used in China.
- 3999 BC - The first 24 hour garage opens in China.
- 3998 BC - The entire Gansu province in China is given over to the production of chocolate-flavoured milk and miniature apple pies.
- 303 AD - Roman Emperor Sodomus woke up and did his thing.
- 1137 - Latin scholar and myopic playboy King Doner the Unwieldy invents the kebab while jousting in the Lake District with friends.
- 1569 - The first National Lottery is launched in England. The 3 groat jackpot is won by our village Marion Stoats who is promptly burnt at the stake for witchcraft. The remainder of the jackpot goes to the Buboe Relief Fund and other good causes.
- 1679 - The British Parliament passed the Habeas Corpus Act, and a couple of huge kidney stones, and a Connecticut license plate.
- 1779 - French forces launch a failed invasion of Britain using boats and swords. Ha hah. Puny bloody foreigners.
- 1898 - Two new moons of Uranus, Rimmar and Scateron, are discovered.
- 1899 - Two more extremely ancient jokes also found circling Uranus.
- 1688 - The Glorious Revolution - William of Orange, becomes King and ends Catholic rule in the UK.
- 1689 - The Fabulous Revolution - Crispin of Pink becomes King and bans bushy eyebrows and those "horrid" firkins.
- 1806 - Isambard Kingdom Brunel born, followed by a huge stovepipe hat. Mother and baby do badly.
- 1840 - In America, medicinal preparations based on cannabis become available, including Cigaweed chewing tobacco, Hempies mouthwash and Bongoloid throat lozenges. Couchlock disease sweeps the nation.
- 1858 - General Walton Clapton Wigfield VI patents a game called 'spharistikionlongousnis'. After some refinement of the rules, and a lie down, it is renamed 'tennis'.
- 1911 - In a saloon, Horace Smith spills Daniel Westerns whiskey. They both reached for their holster and realised they'd have to invent the revolver to settle the score
- 1919 - PT Barnum unveils his latest attraction: The Man With A Child In His Eye
- 1928 - Recreational use of cannabis is made illegal in the UK.
- 1933 - The US And Them becomes the new American flag
- 1938 - The first live radio broadcast of snooker.
- 1934 - Stoners notice.
- 1969 - The Beetles become the first band to have 3 consecutive numbers ones with Please Please Choose Me Or I'll Cry, I'll Kiss All Your fingers One by One, Actually I'm Projecting A Load Of Mother Stuff On You
- 1971 - I was born and my favourite colour is blue.
- 1933 - An 4000 year old emerald lady boy discovered at Wat Thah Fak in southern Thailand
- 1963 - The US was not as war with anyone or any concept.
- 1964 - Nixon declares a war on space.
- 1978 - "I Pity The School", a cartoon starring B-Team star Mr G premiers on US TV. Mr G is the owner of a small Gonzo porn studio where young women visit. Each week he helps them with their sexual maturation. They help him solve mysteries and fight crime. 2 episodes are produced.
- 1979 - The Hamster Wheel by Aghasta Christie becomes the world's longest running play ever.
- 1981 - Ragnar Anton Kitful Fruish Boros Ferrario Aubert Radiziac Wanker III is born.
- 1984 - Schmapple launch their first portable computer. The Lacey III is luggable by two men as long as they have a trolley.
- 1997 - My wife left me for another man.
- 1999 - Russian forces withdraw from Chechnian.
- 2000 - The Millenium Bug cause nearly 0.75 US cents worth of damage worldwide.
- 2002 - Miss Nevada, Angel Dickenson, loses her title after mid-air phone somophore scat orgy footage surfaces (in Estonia)
- 2004 - Data sent from the Galileo Spacecraft Sponsored By Kraft Food, indicates that Jupiter's moon Europa has a liquid ocean enrobed with cheesy white sauce and studded with succulent tuna.
- 2007 - Obsessive blogger N@velGaz0r becomes the first women to circumnavelgaze the world in 27 hours 9 minutes.
- 2008 - Bolloxpedia reaches its one millionth lie.

4000 year old statue

Births   [edit]

- 1956 - Skeletor (born Helmut Skeltar, Greyskall, Illinois)

Deaths   [edit]

On the day in history nobody died. It was beautiful.

Holidays and observances   [edit]

- International Voiceover Day - USA
- Excellence Day - Peoples Republic of China
- National Kumquat Day - Peru

WIGAPEDIA
The Hair-Free Encylopedia

everything you ever wanted to know about
merkins, rugs, pieces, perukes and syrups.

now partnered with

Preserver Limited

An evolving tale 'Humans are not masters of the environment but part of it'

Red Card Gas guzzling cars in pollution clampdown

Get your motor running We nominate 40 essential driving LPs

Today's picks

- Big Brother: Cool but cruel

- Have we had enough of Big Brother?

- Protect our children - ban Big Brother

- Big Brother latest

- Are you angry with Big Brother?

- Can Big Brother save politics?

Friday November 17

Latest: living near a motorway damages children's lungs, research reveals.

Stressed workers cost Europe
One third of workers are suffering from stress, anxiety, depression and cancer.

Extinction looms for fish species
Scientists have called for a worldwide ban on deep-sea trawling following a major report.

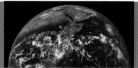

Deadly Blooms
Colombia's flower industry is based on exploitation of its women workers.

More news

Gadgets to drive up emissions
Use of electrical gadgets will raise UK energy consumption by 82% over the next five years.

Flat screens threaten eco-crisis
The energy demands of Britain's obsession with flat televisions could require two nuclear plants.

Environment

The lunacy of our age
Hopping over to New York for a few bargains takes our flying mania to its limit.

Greenpeace steps up 'forest friendly' campaign
Iraq: Greenpeace has enlisted best-selling authors in the latest phase of its drive to urge British publishers to use paper from sustainable sources.

Earth facing 'catastrophic' loss of species
Scientists call for action in biodiversity crisis warning that world faces next mass extinction.

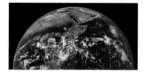

Planet hunter searchse for second Earth
Science: Probe to investigate distant solar systems

CHINAPEDIA
The Information Free Encyclopedia

main page

- Main page

Welcome to Chinapedia

the free encylopedia that no one can edit

1 glorious article extolling the virtue of the glorious Middle Kingdom

Today's featured article

The People's Republic Of China is excellent - an excellent article on how excellent The People's Republic Of China is, was, and always has been.

In the news

China glorious China

Did you know...

...nothing. Carry on. Keep working.

On this day...

Today - The glorious People's Republic Of China continued to develop excellently.

Today's featured picture

Our Glorious Flag

NPOV Disputed Pages

The following pages are currently under dispute regarding their Neutral Point of View (NPOV)

No pages

So here's our glorious flag again.

  Chinationary

  Chinanews

  Chinaquote

  Chinabooks

  Chinaspecies

  Chinasource

amasszone.com   Your Amasszone.com   Software   See All 976898 Product Categories   Your Debt | 🛒 Pile | Your Wants ⊡ ⊡ | Help!

Browse by Incomprehensibility | Complicated | Truly Unfathomable | In Bright Colours | To Make You | Think It's | Easy To Use | When It Isn't

Top Sellers in Software
Updated hourly

1. Mucrosoft Windows Unprofessional **$39.99**
2. Norton Antipasto **$38.95**
3. Mucrosoft Control Freak **$77.95**
4. You Really Should Do Your Tax You Know 1.0 **$86.99**

▸ See more top sellers in Software

Software

Streamline your teens

The ground breaking new features of Mucrosoft Puberty help you manage your adolescence with the minimum of pain and the maximum of strops. Now incorporating WetDreamWeaver, AcneTrack and the latest version of Argumento, a dynamic row generator with built-in artificial intelligence to generate a compendium of surly opening gambits.

Don't get into trouble

Do you really want to look at that page? Do you really want to pull yourself around the room to that? What do you think you're doing, Dave? Just some of the questions ethical firewall software NetConscience interrupts you with as it continuously monitors your traffic and second-guesses your internet decisions.

This Week's Featured Software and Events

Arrest Me Pro
For the paranoid guilt-stricken webuser when the weight of your Internet mis-deeds gets too much. Arrest Me Pro quickly and painlessly dobs your dark ass to the authorities. They'd find out soon enough anyway. So why sweat it out with nightmares and hiding your stash under floorboards etc.
NEW in version 4.0: FairCop(tm) plugin automatically maximises hidden and embarrassing webpages automatically when your spouse or common-law partners enters the room.

Email internet history and cache to

- ☑ my partner
- ☑ the CIA
- ☑ the BBC
- ☐ my grandmother
- ☑ the FBI
- ☐ the tabloids
- ☐ all my friends
- ☑ the Mossad
- ☐ everyone on the internet

Choose who, when and how much of the electronic paper trail to email. (Actual screenshot)

Internet Filter

Fed up with those geeks taking over the Net with their bin/usr talk and their poorly-designed sarcastic newsletters? Yeah us too. That's why Spod Sponge 5 filters out **all** mentions of retro gaming, LOTR, Linux and Japanese food products that sound a bit like 'bum' or 'spunk' from the Internet. Phew!

Before using Spod Sponge 5   After using Spod Sponge 5

Essential software for eggheads everywhere

It's a spreadsheet! It's an ant farm!

Enter data all day long for the rest of your life

Fully featured family edition

Where's My Stuff?
- Right. I'm writing to that program on the telly .
- I've never been treated like this ever.
- Pigs.

Shipping & Returns
- We have some yachts too
- Couple of shiny ones

Need Help?
- Forgotten your children's name? Shit
- Forgotten to take your meds? Schmniff Heeeere
- Visit our Self-Help department.

B-Mail

Introducing B-Mail, the book version of the popular electronic technology used all over the world to rage incoherently at those who have rejected you. Just fill in the blanks on this page, cut out the envelope and send it off into the ether. Exciting isn't it?

B-Mail

Just fill in the recipient, subject line and address and that's it. You've sent your first B-Mail! Delivery is not guaranteed by the way.

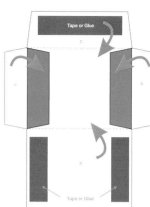

To:

From:

Subject:

Address:

Sark-E-Cards

Mock those less stylish than you. Badger and harangue your work mates. Revel in the failure of a friend. The perfect range of greetings cards for the ironic and ever-so-slightly bitter.

You've had a baby!

How original

OO! A GREAT BIG SHINY EXPENSIVE NEW CAR

TO GO WITH YOUR TINY GREY MOTTLED PENIS

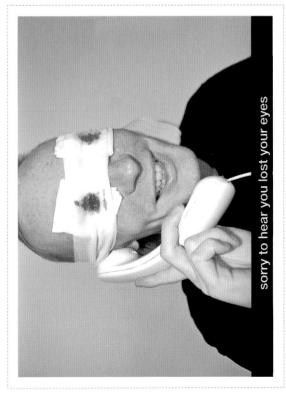

sorry to hear you lost your eyes

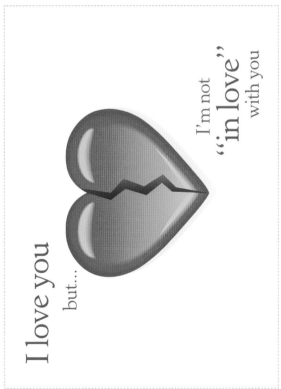

I love you but...

I'm not "in love" with you

Sark-E-Cards

Sark-e-Cards

Sark-e-Cards

Sark-e-Cards

Sark-E-Cards

Yet more cynical felicitations for your friends and enemies to savour.

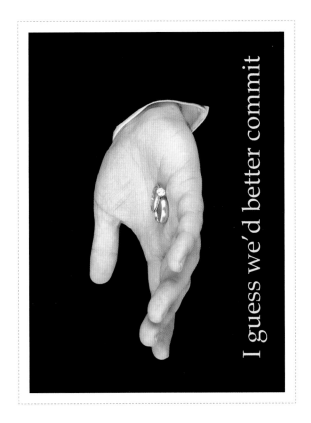

I guess we'd better commit

Happy Realising The Fragility Of Life Day

Hoping You'll Remember Not To Waste Yours!

Congratulations On Your New House Purchase

So glad Mummy and Daddy could help you

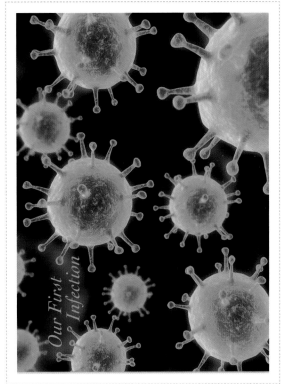

Our First Infection

Sark-e-Cards

Sark-e-Cards

Sark-e-Cards

Sark-e-Cards

Sark-E-Cards

Our final selection is intended for everyday situations in the office and your personal life that require an incisive, unequivocal gesture.

I know where you live

I know where you work

I know what time you wake up

I know what time you go to bed

I know which buses and trains you use

I know your favourite place to have a drink

I know where you like to shop for underwear

I know where all your friends and relations live

I plot your every move on a huge map with coloured pins

Be My Valentine

Wishing You....

A Happy Office Romance!

(like we don't know)

IT'S OVER

Tactless way to do it but hey - welcome to the 21st century.

CONGRATULATIONS!

you're not pregnant

Sark-e-Cards

Sark-e-Cards

Sark-e-Cards

Sark-e-Cards

.com

.com

| Help | Yep | Sold | My Kak | All of it |

Hello! Sign in or register.

All Items   Auctions   Buy It Now

Sign in to see your customized search options

[ ] Search title **and** description

Related Searches :

All Categories [v]   Search   Advanced Search

Matching Categories
Items found for "kak" (82)
Tat
Filth
Kak
Shat
Detritus
Toss
Nonch
Old Stuff
Crap Stuff
Used
   Grubby (122)
   Dented (90)
   Patched up (95)
   Photoshopped (3)
   Stolen
   Thieved
   Nicked
   Palmed
   Had
   Buffed (12)
Loft clinker
Mantel plaque
Rubbish
   In a bag
   In a sack
   In a bit of old net curtain
   Spilling out onto the lino
Of no interest whatsosever
   except to you
   and your sister
   and your mum and dad
   maybe your gran

Handy Guides
How to scour your attic for
   broken crockery
Primer: If it looks worthless,
   it is, but flog it anyway

Search Options
Location:
[ ] In your own shed
[ ] Items in skips within a
   800m radius of your home
Show only:
[ ] Items held together with
   old bits of chewing gum
[ ] Rusting hulks of
   obsolete machinery
[ ] Used items
[ ] Perused items
[ ] Abused items
[ ] Bruised items
[ ] Confused? You're not the
   only one. No-one is really
   sure what's going on here

145,963,700,905,010,002,330,998,342,001,002,854,888 items found for "kak"

• Add to Favorite Searches

💡 Try: • Items found for "kak"

List View | Picture Gallery

Sort by: [v]   Customize Display

[ ] Compare	Item Title	Bids	Price*	Shipping to USA	Time Left ▲

Featured Items

[ ] SHELVING FILE CABINET FILING FILE STORAGE OFFICE
FILING SOLUTION FOR THE FREQUENT FILER IN YOUR LIFE
    — *Have it Now* $380.00 $390.00   Come & get it   1d 23h 56m

Optimize your selling success! Find out how to promote your items

[ ] A Go On My Bike
    1    $20.00   No idea, mate   14m

[ ] Human Placenta (FRESH!)
COME ON HUMANS, YOU KNOW IT MAKES SENSE
    1    $0.99   Not specified   35m

[ ] Lottery Ticket (I've got a good feeling about this one)
    —   *$7.56*   £1000 ish   36m

[ ] Ice Sculpture
HURRY, DEFROSTING
    —   *$3.79*   Not necessary   1h 30m

[ ] HIGGS BOSON (FABLED SUPER PARTICLE FOUND IN MY ATTIC)
    — $29.90   Literally pounds   1h 47m

[ ] TIM BERTIE LEE'S ORIGINAL BLUEPRINTS FOR THE WORLD WIDE WEB
    ▶081   — *Have it Now* $174.99 $179.99   Insert amount   2h 16m

[ ] THE INETRENET NOW IN HANDY BOK FORM by David Mccandliss (Phillipino Pirate Version of the famous book)
    ▶121   — *Have it Now* $174.99 $179.99   Uncertain   2h 18m

[ ] FIGHT CARDS (rare)
THERE'S NO SUCH THING AS FIGHT CARDS
    ▶082   — *Have it Now* $174.99 $179.99   Free!   2h 18m

[ ] Retro Games
USE YOUR FINGERS TO MAKE COMPUTER GO
    ▶080   — *Have it Now* $199.99 $199.99   Rapidly altering   5h 29m

[ ] Shoebox of photos, notebooks and letters from when I was at school / college
    — *Have it Now* $174.99 $179.99   Conditions apply   2h 16m

[ ] Letraset Drawer / filing cabinet in black / white
    — *Have it Now* $174.99 $179.99 $0.01   2h 18m

About Kakbuy | Corporate Kak

kakbUY.com

Video Games > Vintage & Retro Gaming > Other Vintage Gaming > Systems

FEMTO ARCADE 64 - PLAYS ANY VIDEO GAME FROM HISTORY

View lower quality picture

Current bid: **£2.99**   [Place Bid >]

End time: **11-Feb 14:24:53 GMT** (4 days 4 hours)
Postage costs: **£118.40**
Post to: United Kingdom
Item location: County Durham, United Kingdom
History: 2 bids
High bidder: colonic (1)

Meet the seller

Seller: johnathon (498 ☆) [▶102]

Feedback: **1500% Positive** (using HackRatings™)

- Read feedback comments
- Flick through other kak this dude is selling
- Imagine what his house is like
- **God**

Description

The Femto Arcade plays all games from all games consoles from all eras, except the crappy Colecovision, including the type-in games. I'm selling it all with the following:

TomBRAider on the ZX Rainbow

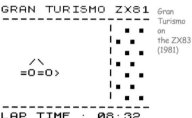

GRAN TURISMO ZX81   Gran Turismo on the ZX83 (1981)

LAP TIME : 08:32
CAR UNLOCKED OPEN MANUAL TO PAGE 82

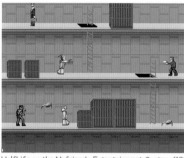

HalfLife on the Nofriendo Entertainment System (1985)

```
10 REM RESIEVIL.BAS by Preston Mucash
20 SCREEN "Black"
30 REM Set weapons
40 WE = 4
00 LET SHOTGUN=0
00 LET SOMECRUDDYPIECEOFPIPE=1
50 REM set amount and position of zombies
60 REM in various buildings around the hero
70 FOR I = 0 TO 12
80 A = 6 - I: PRINT A (I): NEXT
90 REM Calculate zombie intelligence
100 B% = 63 * (1 - .06 * I) : REM viscious
110 G% = 40 * (1 - .06 * I) : REM smarts
120 R% = 45 * (1 - .06 * I) : REM aggression
130 V% = 32 * (1 - 0.6*I): REM distracted one feastine
140 REM generate large box in front of hero which
150 REM is really difficult to climb over
160 PALETTE 3, B% * 65536 + G% * 256 + R%
170 PRINT (320, 320), 3
180 REM initiate lines of dialogue
190 FOR D = 1 TO 5
200 PRINT DATA (D)
210 DATA "Jill, use the key of unlocking things?"
220 DATA "Woah. This town is dangerous."
230 DATA "No you go first. I don't like spiders."
240 DATA "Chris! Your lips!"
250 DATA "Flip the light on. I stubbed my fuckine toe."
260 IF A >= 0 THEN
270 HI = 2 * TH - A
280 LO = -(2 * TH + A)
290 END IF
300 REM Draw the characters
310 PRINT (320, SU), 1, 1
320 PALETTE 1, 334143
330 REM Some lame puzzle involving a gem and a
340 REM alcove on a pillar
350 IF I < 12 THEN CLS
360 NEXT I
370 GOSUB FIGHT
380 GOSUB BLOOD
390 GOTO 10
```

Resident Evil printed in Computron Magazine March 1983

RARE!! Donkey Dong (banned arcade game, 1982)

Tekken IV on the Akari BSE (1982)

MYST

collected 07

Myst on the NoFriendo Gayboy

QUAKE

Quake on The Commander 64 (1981)

Grand Theft Auto v 1.014   Score 5/1000

```
Arnies Guns
It is a gunshop. Everything you could want is right
here within grasp. The shopkeeper asks you what
you would like.

>mug shopkeeper and grab handgun
You flatten the shopkeeper and take the
handgun. Best make a move.

>east
You are standing on the corner of 42nd and
Bridge. You see a gunshop and a ho.

>shoot ho and take money
You shoot the ho with the handgun. She is dead.
You take the $250.

>look
You see a gunshop and a dead ho. Cars pass.
The faint sound of sirens can be heard in the
distance.

>carjack a mutha
You step out into the road and are immediately
run over by an armoured police van.

You are dead.
You scored. 5
Your rating: sux0r

Play again? Y/N
```

Grand Theft Auto The Text Adventure 1987

Ready to bid   help

Item title: Femto Arcade

Current bid: £2.99

Your maximum bid: £ [   ] (Enter £3.19 **or more**)

[Place Bid >] You will confirm in the next step.

Seller's payment instructions
Item will be despatched after cleared payment received.

What else can you do?

◀ | I guess you gotta | Dive in like | Everyone else | And get all that junk out of the attic | Shame you can't sell 70s porn on here | You'd make a killing

Back to a list of kak ◀079 Listed in category: Stolen > Valuable Technical Documents Scribbled By Eggheads > Internet-related >

TIM BERTIES LEE ORIGINAL BLUEPRINTS FOR THE WORLD WIDE WEB

View lower quality picture

Current bid:	£999.999 [Place Bid >]
End time:	11-Feb 14:24:53 GMT (128 days 4 hours)
Postage costs:	£18.40
Post to:	The World
Item location:	The Cayman Islands
History:	99 bids
High bidder:	gullibilitybrown (11)

Meet the seller

Seller: leatherback (001 ☆)

Feedback: **100% Negative** (not using HackRatings™)

- Pick through feedback comments
- Wonder if this guy is a scammer
- Create a suspicion
- **Dob him in**

Description

Unwanted Gift: 96 pages of mostly incomprehensible ramblings from the creator of the 'World Wide Web'. Far too much about his wife and not enough about wires and protocols for my tastes.

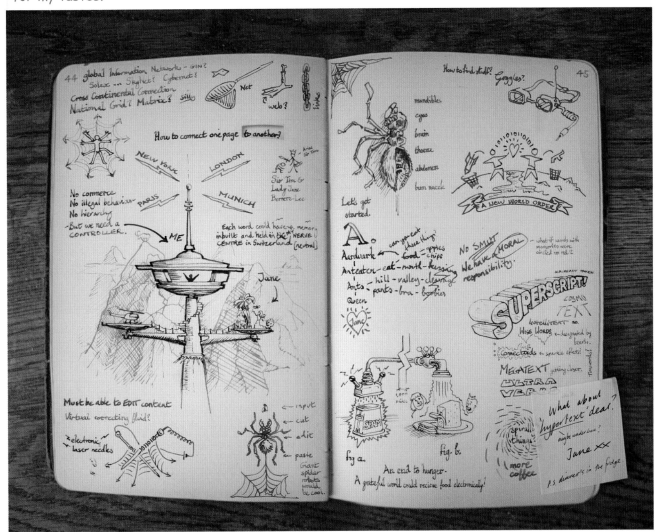

[Place Bid >] You will confirm in the next step.

Seller's payment instructions
Item will be despatched after cleared payment received.

What else can you do?

I could start a business | Doing this | I Could Work From Home | Buying and selling | All Day | That's the life!

◀ Back to a list of kak ◀079 Listed in category: Spoddy Stuff > Cards and kak like that > Battle Cards > These

MY COLLECTION OF SUPER RARE BATTLE CARDS

View a very low quality picture

Current bid: **£42,000** [Place Bid >]

End time: **11-Feb-07 14:24:53 GMT** (4 days 4 hours)

Postage costs: **£18.40**

Post to: United Kingdom

Item location: Spodworthy Rise, Colchester, United Kingdom

History: 900 bids

High bidder: FighterTheManFighter (900)

Meet the seller

Seller: KeepItLight (001☆)

Feedback: **100% Negative (not using HackRatings™)**

▪ How many things am I currently bidding on?
▪ How many am I going to win?
▪ Dive in right at the last second
▪ **That's my tactic**

Description

Ready to bid

help

Item title: SET OF TOP WHACK FIGHTING CARDS

Current bid: £2.99

Your maximum bid: £ [_____] (Enter £3.19 **or more**)

[Place Bid >] You will confirm in the next step.

Seller's payment instructions
Item will be despatched after cleared payment received.

What else can you do?

◀ Stop | Just Stop

THE DULLEST BLOG IN THE WORLD

Sitting on the settee

I was sitting on the settee in my living room. The settee felt quite comfortable to sit on. I continued to sit there for a while.

POSTED BY JEFFREY AT 7:48 PM   900 COMMENTS

Going outside

I was inside my house and decided that I would like to go outside for a while. I picked up my keys, opened the front door and stepped outside. I turned around and closed the door behind me.

POSTED BY JEFFREY AT 8:15 PM   11293 COMMENTS

Putting a piece of junk mail into the recycling box

I discovered a piece of junk mail on my door mat. I carried the item away from the front door and held it above the waste paper basket. I opened my hand, thereby allowing the piece of junk mail to fall into the recycling box

POSTED BY JEFRREY AT 8:17 PM   0 COMMENTS

Taking an item out of a drawer

I opened a drawer by pulling it towards me. I picked up the object I needed and removed it from the drawer. Having done so I pushed the drawer with my hand, thus closing it.

POSTED BY JEFFREY AT 8:53 PM   16 COMMENTS

Taking a sip of coffee

I had a mug of coffee sitting on my desk. I reached out my hand and picked up the mug. I took a sip of coffee before returning the mug to its former position on my desk.

POSTED BY JEFFREY AT 8:55 PM   995 COMMENTS

Turning off a light

A light in one of the rooms of my house was on. I decided that I didn't need the light on any longer. I pressed the light switch thereby turning off the light.

POSTED BY JEFFREY AT 10:05 PM   596 COMMENTS

Crying

Sitting in the dark, I realise that my life was empty. I began to cry. And couldn't stop. I took a tissue from the draw and wiped my eyes. I threw the tissue in the bin, lay my head on the desk and continued to sob.

POSTED BY JEFFREY AT 10:30 PM   0 COMMENTS

MY FAVOURITE BLOGS

Manty's Borscht Diary

Drabster

Ditchwasser

Snoozearama

Bore De Jour

Trite Overload

boringboring.net

WilWheaton.net

Poormatch Profile

Contradictory? Moi?
vacillate wildly

Active within 24 hours
29-year-old woman seeking very patient men 29-36

About Me

I like going out and staying in, cheap wine and expensive lager, and wearing my hair both up and down. I like black and white arthouse and mushy squishy technicolour chick flicks, chintzy sofas and Scandinavian minimalism, eco-friendly bicycles and driving around in my tank, working out obsessively and then stuffing myself full of cakes, dressing like a princess and then letting the hair on my legs grow, dogs and then cats, cats then dogs, city breaks and walking in the country ...there's never a dull moment in my kooky corner of the world. Come fly (or maybe drive, what about swimming? We could just walk. Let's take a tram! No I want to stay curled up on the sofa with a bottle of wine and a DVD) with me!

About who I'm looking for

Someone with the patience of a saint and the hands of a bus driver.

More about me

Occupation:	Beauty therapist, nurse, child minder , travel journalist
Favourite animal?	Hamster
Height:	No, gazelle.
Weight:	No, actually, caribou. They have cute noses.
Eyes:	Are we still on the animal question?
Perfect Date:	I think Horse. Definitely a horse.

Poormatch Profile

PrickTease
Take me - I'm yours. Perhaps.

Active all the time baby
21-year-old woman seeking charismatic masterful men 79-99!

About Me

I may look sweet, innocent and incredibly pert, but believe me, I have a ravenous hunger. I am insatiable. My body is supple; I like to take care of it all – breasts, nipples, thighs, and of course labia – majora AND minora. If this kind of talk arouses you, you're not alone. Many men have emailed me. My box is full. If you would like to take your place inside my box, go ahead.

About who I'm looking for

I'm looking for an adventurous lover who can match me, thrust for thrust. Someone who can make my body twang like a Jew's harp and rattle like a snaredrum. He must be rich and well-turned out and close to death.

More about me

Height:	6'2"
Ankle:	Bracelet
Currently wearing:	Very little
How little?	Very little indeed
What, like, a thong?	Smaller than that.
Body type:	Perfect
Favourite Food:	Men, Coquette potatoes
Religion:	My faith is very important to me and I believe that sex should only be enjoyed by a loving and committed couple within the confines of a stable marriage and for the sole purpose of procreation.
What could be smaller than a thong FFS?	Marry me and you'll see.

Poormatch Profile

SportTilly
Run!

Active every minute of everyday
31-year-old woman seeking cross-fit over-pronators 26-48

About Me

Like hiking up mountains, orienteering to the summit, paragliding down, going kayaking in the river at the bottom and then spear-fishing for my supper. I will tell you that I've yet to meet anyone who can tame me. I am nearly 7 foot tall in my heels, so only tall gents who don't mind public emasculation need apply. I belong to a hockey club, go running and am ;h part of the UK Women's Cage Fighting 7. I am also a keen yachtswoman and am hoping to be the first woman to sail around the world with just one Kate Bush tape.

That said, at the end of hard days combat, I like nothing better than curling up on the sofa with a glass of red wine and a DVD.

About who I'm looking for

I'm looking for a good solid man to do lots of very sporty things with. An over-pronator most likely. He mustn't be a spectator. He must be out there, hopping, skipping and jumping into the sand pit of life. Some experience of martial arts and breaking submission holds useful.

More about me

Height:	6"1'
Width:	4"5'
Occupation:	Trainee Psychotherapist
Favourite Animal:	The Hamster
Favourite Bodypart:	The neck

Poormatch Profile

VodkaFairy
Go on then I'll have another, make that two

Active within 1 hour
24-year-old woman seeking drunks, alcoholics, and frustrated artists 18-26

About Me

I like to have a drink, just socially, well, socially at first, before moving on to more committed and hardcore boozing. I find it helps me to relax, and then, after a couple more, it helps me to function like a human being. Where would I be without booze? Hello?

I also like lying face down on the sofa with several bottles of red and a DVD.

About who I'm looking for

Ideally, they would be moderate to heavy drinkers, with the ability to drink me under the table, and then pick me up from under the table to pour another drink in my mouth. If we can remember a single detail of our courtship, I'd say we've failed.

More about me

Starsign:	Smirnoff
Weight:	Bantam
Lips:	Like cherry wine
Drink:	Very kind of you - double Amaretto please
Perfect date:	Meet at a poorly chosen bar just after work, get drunk due to nerves, followed by wretched smeary throwaway sex just to feel alive
What's on my bookshelf?	Errrrrrrrmmmm [sounds of crashing]

note: poormatch.com cannot be held responsible for fun you might have distributed yourself across this site
poormatch.com is a wholly under the thumb of Bahoogle.com

The worst dating site in the world

Poormatch Profile

Darren
Up for it

Active mostly late at night
29-year-old man seeking a torrid French-style affair with mistress (24-48)

About Me

I'm tall, successful, loving, kind, funny, open and a great cook, but only available for dates on the weekday evening or very quickly at lunch time. It's been a while since I felt loved, or understood, or listened to, or just felt ALIVE you know? I long for those moments after you've made long, shabby, usery love in a cheap hotel room and are lying in the crook of each others' arms, staring at the ceiling, feeling all hollow and ... and...you know I can't keep it in anymore. And why should I??? You seem like a good listener. My wife. She - I don't know, she doesn't seem to want me anymore. The light has gone off in her eyes. We used to touch and frott slightly while making breakfast but not anymore. Most nights we would passionately flick through our wedding photos or we'd watch our feature length wedding video with the soundtrack of Lord Of The Ring Wars in the background (for grandeur). But now it's a once a week job, if that. I've tried crying. I've tried begging. I've tried turning up randomly at her work with a spanish guitar and a battery-operated amplifier and serenading her in front of all her executive media mates. But she doesn't respond. She looks at me, ashamed. It's like she doesn't know me. Do you know what I mean? You're different to her though. Softer. Anytime, see you next week? Same time. No don't call. I'll text you.

About who I'm looking for

A good listener with a silly streak and no baggage. Someone available lunchtimes and weekday evenings.

More about me

Interests:	drinking, smoking, playing video games
Eyes:	What?
Work:	Recently made redundant
Perfect Date:	few beers, watching Lord Of The Ring Wars
Outlook:	can't complain, mustn't grumble

Poormatch Profile

DefenderOfTheRealm
It's dog eat dog chum

Active within 24 hours in any hotspot in the world
45-year-old man seeking amoral women 26-48

About Me

My life as an arm's dealer has allowed me to travel the world and come into contact with all different types of cultures and their refugees. As a result I can talk about almost anything... God, life, death, pens, liverspots, rimming, The Smiths, chopsticks, dirt.

Life is about openness, I've learnt, seeing things from both sides of the barbed-wire fence. Hence i don't like people who are narrow-minded and judge others. If that's you, stop reading now. I don't want you around me.

About who I'm looking for

Svelt, sociable, well-educated woman as happy hosting a dinner-party for diplomat's wives as she is hosing down a middle-man in a Nairobi backstreet to secure a deal.

More about me

Interests:	landmines, fragmentation grenades, uranium casings - that sort of thing

Poormatch Profile

MasterfulCock
That got your attention, didn't it?

Active within 24 hours
30-year-old woman seeking wanton uberbabes 8.5-9.5 out of ten.

About Me

So you're that type of girl huh? That's good because I regard myself as a dominant and skilled lover. I've finessed my knowledge with a good deal of Gonzo pornography, and am now looking for someone with low self esteem to practice on. Date one will involve my ordering for you in a restaurant; date two with your being handcuffed to a radiator while I call you a whore. I like to be addressed as 'Sir', but you can call me 'Daddy' on your birthday. And if you're a very good girl and don't cause too much fuss I'll get you to remake my bed with hospital corners.

I work as an actor and gigilo, making elderly rich ladies feel special by wearing a tuxedo and serving my penis up to them in a silver cigarette case which I have cut the bottom out of. You like? Good. My days consist of lounging around town with my actor mates, smoking cigarettes and talking about conquests and male grooming products.

About who I'm looking for

Oh I don't know. Someone who likes to laze around playing with their genitals while I film it on my phone? Best not to be prescriptive at this stage ... let's start with mutual attraction and some nude photos and take it from there.

More about me

Interests:	Collecting Internet sextapes
Job:	Making Internet sextapes
Eyes:	Come to bed
Favourite pasttime :	Getting my leg over and my arm in up to the elbow
Perfect Date:	Cocktails at the Ritz, lavish dinner with friend, frottage in the back of a cab, a lot of dirty talk, the deed, long shower
My favourite possessions:	My HD handicam

Poormatch Profile

Bloody Women
Oh what's the point?

Active within 24 hours
37-year-old man seeking any idiot woman

About Me

Moaning, angry, desperate. That's me. So what? Dating is a waste of time. My girlfriend left me six years ago and I'm pretty much over it. I still collect my faeces to send to her but I only actually post it when I remember now, which my dad says is an improvement. My mum doesn't like it of course. But then what a surprise! What does she like? What has she ever liked? Apart from shopping. And talking and nagging. Do this. Do that. Wash this. Wipe that.

About who I'm looking for

I don't really have a checklist but if I was honest I can generally only relate to young women, very young women, preferably who don't speak much English and who don't mind a bit of slap and tickle. The less baggage the better. No sexual health issues. No nags. No indecisive types. Enjoy snuggling in front of some hardcore pornography.

More about me

Interests:	mulling over all the time I've ever been hurt
Job:	Minicab driver
Eyes:	Hard
Perfect Date:	No such thing
Outlook:	Cloudy
My favourite possessions:	A set of watertight jiffy bags and a box of surgical gloves

you requested some pop-up ads

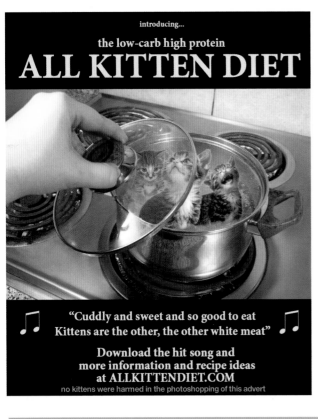

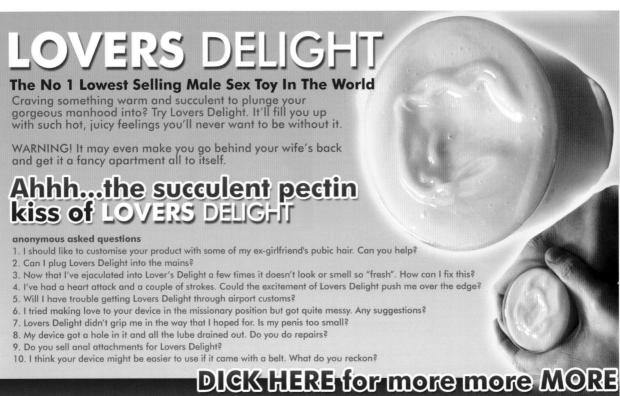
like ads? find more <u>here</u>   050   117

mineminemyplace
a place for yourself and no one else

Myhome | MyPeople | MyWeb | MyMusic | MyBlogs | MyVideo | MyCommunity | MyLife | MyWorld | MyOpinions | Mine! | Mine! | All Mine

Cool New Videos

52,083 uploaded today!

Me Dancing
Me

Me Talking
Me

Mum Talking
About Me

Guess who?
Yeah

the nightmare continues...

**Did you know ...
somewhere in the world
at this moment
a beautiful
but poor child
is dying
because of you?**

Guilt
International

support our new campaign

MAKING YOU CRY

MineMineMyPlace Music

[more music]

Shaman Me

Drums/Percussion/Ambient Crap
UK

It's not just superb layer-upon-layer of drums and percussion by Shaman Steve Chomley-Formonderly (buffalo drums, udu pots, seed pods, horses, margerine tubs, commodore 64s, and a little penny whistle from a christmas cracker). These are fundamental if not magical atmospheric textures. It's like one organic breathing, thinking, feeling, sensing entity enveloping utterly so that you feel you're flying through the solar winds of the Rigus Nebula. No words can express except perhaps "Wow! Got any more of those pills hon?"

Cool New People Who Aren't Me

Mandisa   Hevs   jodes

Video EXCLUSIVE!

[more videos]

Me
Director: Me
Running Time: 4 hours
A characterful one camera piece showing me pottering around the house, making sly observations and sitting in silence watching the day hove past my window.

MineMineMyPlace Specials

Men Of MineMineMyPlace Calendar

And not just the handsomes ones! The cream of the crop of social community hunks. Muttons, sportoids, troll, geeks, leatherettes, doggers, groomers, convicted sex pests, sweaties, bong nancies, croaksters, indie gays, fonzies, L7s, factoids, jocks. Flavours galore.

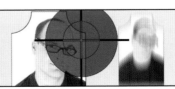
MineMineMyPlace is one of a Bahoogle.com's top friends

mineminemyplace
a place for yourself and no one else

Browse Users

Set Browse Criteria

Basic **Advanced**

Browse For:
- ( ) Women
- ( ) Men
- ( ) Both

between ages:
18 and 18

who are:
- [ ] Single
- [ ] Self Obsessed
- [ ] Single because they're self-obsessed

level of disillusionment with this stuff
- [ ] Low
- [ ] High
- [ ] Very high
- [ ] All-consuming

located within:
Country: United Kingdom
Postal Code: Any miles from

photos:
Show only users who are hott [✓]

Sort Results By: ( ) Recently Updated ( ) Last Login ( ) Naiviety

Update

1 2 3 4 5 >> 75   Next >

Search Results

Davros	What?	Azeroth	Free As A Bird	HappyGirl1982

Shit	Nopleaseno	Graphic Designer	Geoffrey Hollow	Paracetemol & Shandy

Chuckles	FluffyBunny	QueenL	OiOi	BassRush

1 2 3 4 5 >> 75   Next >

MineMineMyPlace has messaged Bahoogle.com, like, eight times and that pecker still hasn't replied

MINEMINEMYPLACE MUSIC

Tokyo Ritz
Pop / Club / Hip Hop

"The Official Tokyo Ritz MySpace Page"

California
United States

Profile Views: 5633861

View My: Pics | Videos

Contacting Tokyo Ritz

 It can fly!

 You're so short

 G+? What's G+?

 Stab with bent sword

 Ah. Tick a folder

Feel a bit up and down

Tokyo Ritz's Friends Comments

Displaying 50 of 79666 comments (View All | Add Comment)

Dj/Producer Ricky King

Online Always!

24 Feb 5:01

Hi Tokyo Ritz, Thanks for the add! just wanted to invite u to a party at my place. It's going to be good. My mum's ourt and all my friends'll be there. Just reply for guest list and the address.

Speak soon
Rick

Shaman Me

24 Feb 2:45

Hey you. Thanks for the add! Was good talking to you yesterday even if you culdn't reely hear wot I sayin becuz you were on stage and I wuz at home using mindrays and a chalk pentagram to speak inside your brian. Cu bout 4 weeks. xxxxxxxxxxxxxxxxxxxxxx

HottGrllll

24 Feb 1:48

Thanks for the add! DO U THINK I'M HOTT? U B THE JUDGE. (no more nasty messages plz)

Suzie

Johnathon

24 Feb 0.52

Hey Tokyo. Thanks for the add! I need to point out however that you have several HTML inconsistencies and one JAVASCRIPT error on this page. There are some alignment issues with a couple of the images which you can fix if you switch to XHTML 1.0.5. I can do this for you. Just msg back your number and I call to arrange a time.

Hungry Man

24 Feb 4.20

Thanks for the add! Dinner?

Spanktasm Plays: 2614313
Download | Rate | Watch The Video!

No, Give Me The Tape Plays: 2614313
Download | Rate | Comments | Lyrics | Add

Tokyo Ritz's Latest Blog Entry [Subscribe]

Celebrate Tokyo's Birthday With Her! Tickets for the restricted view, non-celebrity holding pen still available. Only $99 dollars each. (view more)

Tokyo in Only Sugar And Spice Magazine!
The number 1 mag for 12 year old girls (view more)

Tokyo at the Music Awards. Don't forget to catch Tokyo backstage chuckling at the word "snog" (view more)

Toyko On The Tomorrow Show. Head down to Times Square and cheer limply in the rain (view more)

[view all blog entries]

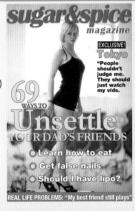

About Tokyo Ritz

Tokyo Ritz is an internationally-celebrated actress, singer, celebrity, socialite, party girl, inn-keeper, heiress, lion-tamer, eating champion, plastic surgeon, spokeperson, writer, actress, did we say that, yes and adult performer.

[more]

Tokyo Ritz's Friend Space. Tokyo Ritz has 15277189 friends. All real.

Barron Nico Ritz IV

Hassel Davidoff I

Doctor Ciagra 852-SCRIP

Prince Fasad Al Fadad XI

King Zombie

2Hott4U

Princess Excellent IV

Naughty Grrrl XXX

View All Of Tokyo Ritz's Friends

MineMineMyPlace.com thanks Bahoogle.com for the add!

mineminemyplace
a place for yourself and no one else

Myhome | MyPeople | MyWeb | MyMusic | MyBlogs | MyVideo | MyCommunity | MyLife | MyWorld | MyOpinions | Mine! | Mine! | All Mine

your name

photo

snappy sassy subtitle

details

View My: Pics | Videos

Contacting your name

Your name's **Interests**

General

Music

Movies

Television

Books

Your name is in your extended network

Your name's **latest blog entry**

Your name's **blurbs**

Your name's **friends**

Your name's **comments**

design your own page

BLOG ENTRIES

Try to keep these as inane as possible. Or self-consciously quirky. That works too. If you're short on ideas, here are some to try.

• I'm a little bit tired. I think I might go to sleep now.

• Urgh I don't know what to write. Have you got any ideas?

• Bought an accordion today. Don't know why.

• Charismatic ultrafauna rims the multiverse.

• Sorry. Was high on paint stripper when I posted that.

• Are you manifesting your presence right now???

• Dull quizzy thing I found

• Jeez. Why did I start this page?

KᴿAZY KᴡESTIᴼNNAIᴿE

Wot r u like? Ever wondered? Kewl then. Answer this krazy qwestions kompiled by top boffins and then upload them to your profile! Hongu!

• What did u listen to right then?
• What colour was your last stool?
• If you were a crayon, what animal would you most resemble?
• Is it snowing?
• Oh why not?
• What is colour right now?
• What's the first thing the opposite sex notice about your tits?
• Ever got so drunk you threw up through your nose and then slept with a small dog like a poodle or perhaps a schnauser?
• Favourite month?
• Favourite second of the day?
• Hugs or thumps?
• Kisses or pisses?
• Tea or pee?

CHECKLIST

Designed your page? Great. Now to make it as eye-popping as possible, be sure to hit as many items on this checklist as possible.

photos
- ◉ only half your face showing
- ○ making gang sign
- ○ better looking friend in picture
- ○ drunk
- ○ out clubbing in a silly hat
- ○ eating flies

about me blurb
- ◉ "Cor! Never done anything like this before"
- ○ More exclamation marks than ideas!!!!!
- ○ Love love love
- ○ Something about body piercings
- ○ And tatoos

general profile
- ◉ Play shit music track without asking
- ○ Crash browser
- ○ Fourteen pages high
- ○ Comic Sans MS
- ○ 19 YouFlue clips stacked ontop of each other in one big processor dragging skyscraper
- ○ Ironic placement of William Shatner in your friends list
- ○ Crash browser again
- ○ page views: 19

HIDEOUS BACKDROPS

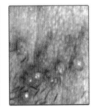

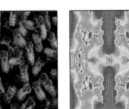

CRAP FLYER FOR YOUR MATE'S PARTY

kak night out

::: WAREHOUSE-STYLE PARTY IN THE BACK OF A BAR :::

SAT 31st MAY / 19 Islet Of Langhans Approach, St Albans

DISCO/TECHNO/CLASSICAL/COUNTRY/PLINKYPLONK/SPEED/AFRICANDRUMMING

MC PLECTAR AKA ALLAN SEABOLD, 45 AINSLEY ROAD, GRIMSBY::::::::::::

ZAC POUDRE (KAK RECORDS)::

MY BROTHER'S SISTER'S MATE (HE HAD THESE LIGHTS WE NEEDED RECORDS)::::::

NASTEE BOI, CHEAKY GRL, AND THE DYLEXIA KREW::::::::::::::::::

GARISH COLOUR SCHEMES

Vorn

Woot?

Ipcres

Sputum

Girlie

Rage, Rage

For example mineminemyplace pages created with our DIY system, visit http://www.theinternetnowinhandybookform/mineminemyplace

Police Signs
4 photos / 0 views

Sets | Tags | Archives | Favorites | Popular | Profile

East Dulwich, South London

Peckham, South London

Forest Hill, South London

Brixton, South London

AMERICA'S MOST WANTED VACATIONS

Florida   Aspen   Las Vegas   Grand Canyon   Vacations Outside The Homeland

Find Me The Best Priced Trip!

◉ Flight + Hotel   ◯ Hotel Only
a 'flight' means travelling by aeroplane

From: [   ]   To: [   ]

Depart: [mm/dd/yyyy]   [Morning ▼]

Return: [mm/dd/yyyy]   [Evening ▼]

Lateness: [hh/mm/ssss]   [Very ▼]

Travellers: [1 ▼]   Width: [Jumbo ▼]

Screaming Annoyance Units (aged 0-8) [1 ▼]

No. of in-flight meals: [1 ▼]   Frequency: [1 ▼]

Hotel in a Different City, Last Minute Deals

Haggle Like You Mean It
No matter that you could buy the entire village if you wanted. Haggle with starving market traders and rickshaw drivers until they cry. Bargains galore!

Speak with one of our experts
Not her though.
She's too good-looking

Chocky   Mogadon   Mt Slipper
CLIMB THE MOUNTAIN AND THEN COME DOWN AGAIN

TWO WEEK ROMANTIC CRUISE
watching our deluxe liner disgorge its sewage into the sunset

Despotic Friends Of America Holiday

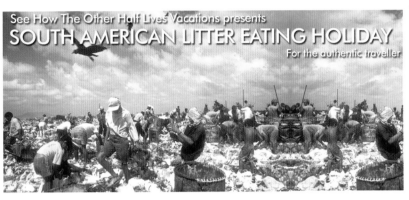

14 day undemocratic nation tour

EGYPT - LIBYA - SINGAPORE - GEORGIA (US STATE)

Luxury sea-facing compounds from $9500 a day

See How The Other Half Lives Vacations presents
SOUTH AMERICAN LITTER EATING HOLIDAY
For the authentic traveller

Featured Vacations

Luxury Dubai!
Stay at the luxurious ten star Al Arabia Hotel on a diamond encrusted penisula. Sleep on a mattress stuffed with slaves. Enjoy a simulation of the entire universe in your room.

Singapore
Savour the sights and delights of the right wing Eastern paradise. Watch what you say. Don't chew gum. And definitely don't be gay. Otherwise enjoy your stay! $999

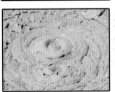

Primeval Soup Holidays
Grub around in the muck like the overgrown guppy you truly are. Rest your vestigal limbs in the volcanic mud.

Turkey
Don't worry about the human rights record, corrupt police, lack of press freedom and ethnic cleansing of the Kurds - just look at the colour of that bloody sea.

Least Popular
Nudist Beach, Darfur
Pony-Trekking, Bahgdad
Italian Cooking, PyongYang
Water-water rafting, Rwanda
Fruit-picking, Angola
Litter-picking, Lebanon
Political Play Writing Course, Tibet

Shyeeeet! It's the The whole entire world

see if you can work out how to use our interactive map to book your vacation
▶ 094

NULLAIR.COM
THE NO FARES AIRLINE

yup, we pay you to travel with us

AMERICAN MAP OF THE WORLD

OIL

CANADA

AUSTRALIA

THE RHOMBUS OF EXCELLENCE

THE GLORIOUS
UNITED STATES
OF
AMERICA

SCOTLAND,
LONDON

IRELAND,
LONDON
our freedom
fighting brothers

HUGH GRANT
HOUSE

JAPAN

LONDO

TOP
DRAWER
WEED

CIGARS

KEY

- ■ Evil
- ■ Goodies
- ■ Baddies with oil, so honourary Goodies
- ■ Ours
- ■ Will be ours soon
- ■ Don't know and don't care
- ■ Will be underwater soon so who gives a frig?
- ■ Got no idea
- ■ Let's go shopping

GAK

COKE

C C C

SNOW

COCAINE

PERCY

BOLIVIAN

SNOW

TOOT

CHARLIE

BEAK

405 This page in the sequel

The page you are looking for will be appearing in the next edition of
The Internet Now In Handy Book Form! It may have been too ahead
of its time, been a less funky page that needed to be sacrificed to
allow a funkier page to come in. Or perhaps it was just left on a
shelf somewhere. Oopsie.

Please try one of the following:

- Close this book, wait a year or so then buy the sequel.
- Visit http://www.theinternetnowinhandybookform.com where you
  will find an electronic version of the book with extra pages.
- Turn ⇦ Back to the previous page and then reopen this page
  once more.

PTTP 405 - Page in sequel
The Internet Now In Handy Book Form!

"I go home. I brush my teeth. Then I go to bed. Usually in pyjamas. Sometimes just in my pants"
Hassel Davidoff

NOTBITCH

```
                                    23.02   ISSUE 001
```
Free every week: to subscribe/unsubscribe
go to http://www.notbitch.com

* A horrible story about someone sexually abusing an animal
* Mother-brother connections
* charts: somebody is number one!

>> Wash me up before you go go! <<
        Be careful with that dryer

    Which moderately succesful singer allegedly used the
    toilets of a mid-priced restaurant to perform a bodily
    function? Our mole revealed: "She went into the
    cubicle alone, locked the door, and proceeded to defecate
    or perhaps urinate. She then washed her hands and just
    walked away without a word."

Who got her big break on American TV when she was spotted in an
audition by a casting director?

>> Big Questions <<
        What people are asking this week.

    Which two Mancunian stadium rockers regularly share a
    mother?

    Which well known actor is renowned in some circles for
    liking to insert his penis into his wife during sex?

Gruesome twosome, Sharon Ouzobourne and Ozzie Ouzobourne.

 >> Twice as much sugar <<
        Be careful with that dryer

    Which two hieress sisters have had a long-term
    relationship with a man twice their age? They've been seen
    out buying presents and even staying over at weekends,
    sometimes both at the same time. And their nickname for
    him? 'Daddy'.

Which former Big Brother star has been visiting private schools
looking for places for her children?

>> Corporate Whores <<
        Bands up for the highest bidder

    Rock'n'roll died a long time ago if rumours coming out
    of the music industry are correct. A slew of top name
    rock acts can now be bought by anyone with a fat
    cheque and a field. Bob Dylon, Radiodread, Roberta
    Williams and 15 Cent have all taken up these lucrative
    offers to 'headline' at payola concerts overseas.

"David Peckham outside the VIP area of Arsenal football club
drinking beerwhile sitting down and watching football."

spodwire

A DIRECTORY OF VERY GEEKY THINGS

Search Spodwire

FRIDAY, NOVEMBER 17, 2007

You Know You've Been Using Your Laptop Too Much When...

Hilarious list from the readers of Gonty Gonty.

1. You stare at the corner of your newspaper to check the time.
2. You call your new child '802.11n' or 'superdrive' (if it's a girl).
3. You use two fingers to scroll down your wife's clitoris.
4. ...or you press down on it for 5 seconds to reboot if she freezes.
5. You try to fold up the TV and take it to your bedroom to watch 24.
6. In a coffee shop, you ask the staff to look after your newspaper when you go to the toilet.
7. Your reason for leaving the toilet-seat up is that you've still got some downloads going.
8. You buy an extra padded bag to carry your diary around in safety and comfort.
9. Instead of boasting about the wild place you've had sex, you brag about strange venues where you've checked email.
10. You've given it a cat-like name like Lappy, you take it to bed with you, and IT wakes YOU up in the morning by purring in your ear.
11. You're blogging live from your grandmother's open casket.

posted by Cory at 08:16:17 AM permalink | blog's comments

The New Zombie Films

THE MUD, THE MUSIC, THE MUUUUAAAAGGGH...

GLASTZOMBIE

AIM FOR THE HEADLINERS

Coming August 2007
to a field near you

News reaches us of a new Zombie films soon to shuffling its way to the big screen. It sounds way cool: Link (Thanks DJ Solomon)

posted by Cory at 08:16:18 AM permalink | blog's comments

Rude Fonts

Gylnn says: "Here are some rude fonts I'm developing for a web project. I just thought I'd share." Good fun. Some of these sound way cool: Link

Anal
Anal Black
Anal Rounded Bold
Comic Glans MT
Century Schoolboy
Courier Nude

HattenScheisser
Lucida Caligula
New Pork
Symbollocks
WingDongs

posted by Cory at 08:16:20 AM permalink | blog's comments

Worse Things That Can Happen To You While Online Dating

Visitors to Poormatch.com have come up with these horror moments. Link
• your mum winks you
• your dad winks you
• the admin removes you pic: "too ugly"
• your work colleagues discover your profile and the picture of you in your pulling shirt, photocopy it onto A3 sheets and paste it liberally around your workplace
• your work colleague discover the fake girl profile you put up to "experiment", photocopy it onto etc

posted by Cory at 08:16:23 AM permalink | blog's comments

datr♥
the hi-tech way to find, meet and have other people

Why leave your romantic choices to chance when a great big computer can make them for you?

What is datr?

Only the most advanced dating site on the planet. Using our unique, patented technologies, you can find trillions of like-minded singletons from all over the world.

What can it do?

How long you got? Just upload your profile and start tracking:
- how long potential partners browsed your profile
- which pictures they looked at and how many times
- who they looked at before, after and simultaneously
- whether they printed it, showed it to other people and laughed

Why?

Whoops. Sorry. Seem to have run out of space down this side to explain that .

Searchr [   ]

over 10,967,000,0013 profiles around the world

DesireTrack™ Platinum

Using Face Recognition technology, the latest developments in cognitive neuro-pyschology and the Hubble Endoscope, we can now build an exact photo-profile fit of your ideal DesireMate™.

Don't be put off by this gruesome potato person. This e-fit represents the core facial components of your ideal mate *as perceived by your brain.* You can increase resolution and fit accuracy by uploading pictures of your mother, father, siblings, ex-partners and any creepy uncles you had floating around during your childhood.

The resulting endo-desire skeleton is then exo-mapped over all newly uploaded profile portraits within your catchment and then simul-tracked and cross-referenced with your interests and personality criteria and mixed in a cauldron with a big spoon. These results are then used to suggest possible targets you will find attractive before you even know it yourself.* It's like Logan's Run, it really is.

(We were kidding about the cauldron BTW. It's more of a vat).

DateRate™

Realtime feedback forms and evaluation matrices allow partners to be constantly updated across a range of key dating metrics

dating	appearance	play	sex	aftermath
☑ chatting	☑ clothes	☑ kissing	☑ sex (full)	☑ pillow talk
☑ flirting	☑ smile	☑ dirty talk	☑ blowjob / cunni	☑ guest towels
☑ punctuality	☑ bod	☑ steamy emails	☑ undressing skills	☑ guest gown
☑ similar to photo?	☑ hair	☑ inventiveness	☑ contraceptive use	☑ SMS ability
☑ follow up	☑ teeth	☑ fingering	☑ anal okay?	☑ mental stability

Additional Features

Our engineers have spent years refining, testing and then refining more and more features for you to use in your romantic quest.

 Monetise Your Profile All artists listed under the 'music tastes' can be linked to the Apple Music Store for a referral percentage on any sales. Books are linked to Amasszone.com: any sexual interests to AdultDVDs.com.

 OriginalityScan (tm) Our server AI backreferences the opening emails your approachee is sending against others they have sent. Duplication, templating, multi-posting or other creepiness can be detected.

 StalkGuard Use our custom, industrial strength barring technologies to block a person from emailing you; block a range of IPs from seeing your profile, or to send a SWAT team of Chechnyans armed with pipes to rough the wacko up a bit (StalkGuard Premium only).

 ScrapeWorldIdealMateATron (tm) Siphons data from all other dating sites in the Kosmos looking for ideal matches.

 MingFilter (tm) Licensed from PoorMatch.com, this face recognition technology strips your search results of uglies, fuglies, OMFuglies, potato-people and hunchbacks upstream.

 STItrack By cross-referencing user data with medical records at sexual health clinics we are able to track common sexual infections across our users and alert any potential partners to this threat by draping a huge red 'LURGEE' sign over their profile.

---

*Members of datr are legally obliged to date the results of a DesireTrack™ Platinum match up. See our Terms & Conditions

---

After six months of emailing and a lot of deep messaging Datr.com is now in a committed exclusive relationship with Bahoogle.com

---

HackersDIY
making stuff that does stuff out of stuff

| Blog | Evil | Gobcasts | Mad Projects | FFS! | Buy stuff |

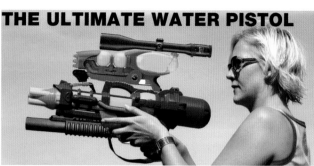

THE ULTIMATE WATER PISTOL

- Infrared scope
- Pump action
- 300 psi water-bomb delivery
- Pneumatic relay solonoids
- Whatever they are
- 1500m range
- Nice colours
- Girl not included

Blog

Make your own Harrier Jump Jet

Vertical aerial liftoff has never been easier to achieve in the garage. All you need are a couple of old filing cabinets, a length of piano wire and a lot of fireworks. Read More

James Bond-style Laser Castrator

Got any laser pointers lying around? If they're still legal in your country, gaffer tape around 400 into a single cannon, then attach them to a pool table tilted around 32 degrees (They used a table at 35 degrees in the film but we tried it and you actually slip off. Those fakers!)... Read More

Hadron Particle Accelerator

The Chonk. Davros Dot. Lactar. Track down those ever-elusive quantum particles in your bathroom with just a few toilet rolls, a bicycle pump and some fireworks. We show you how. Disclaimer: we cannot be held responsible for any singularities, explosions or gaps in the space time continuum generated by this hack. Read More

Blood, sweat and fears

Want to be an expressionless, non-smoking pussy master? Thought so. Try our easy, relatively dangerous tutorials for making nicotine patches, herbal viagra, and botox out of everyday household ingredients. Read More

Home Lobotomy Kit

When Rego bricks and internet friends just aren't enough to make you feel real, end it all effortlessly and horribly in a snap. All you need is a couple of forks, a drill, a bowl and an old tv. Guaranteed to put you in the dead zone. Read More

DIY Jet Skateboard

Who needs legs or skillz? Not you. Just a handful of magnets, four shopping trolley wheels, a plank, a hair-dryer and some fireworks will have headz turning down at the local pitztop. True dat! Read More

Podcasts

Pimping The Schmapple Micro

In the latest episode, radical hacker Pat Mckirk shows how to fit Schmapple's tiny computer to anything: to your phone, in your shower, or even to a spade for essential iTuna streaming while doing garden chores. Read More

Hall Of Bloody Mirrors

You've heard of hacking a Mac to run PC software? Well how about this. We take a Mac and run Windows on it. In Windows we run a Mac-emulator which is running a copy of Windows and has a Mac-emulator running a PC-emulator of Mac. Descend Into A Spiral Of Infinity

Projects

Invasion Of The Body Snatchers
Generate alien invasion hysteria in your hick town. Make your own alien spores and pods, photorealistic dead bodies, and screaming, pointing people Read More

JKEA Hackz
Did you know if you take the plinth from the Strombo cupboard and two metal rods from the Lordstrom shelf units and various other parts from your local JKEA store, you can easily fashion a huge walking talking robot that fires lasers. Read More

Regulars

EVIL GEEK

In this week's column Erwin Malevolent shows kids how to kill ants the 21st century way. He tells them how a USB-powered magnifying glass hooked into a BigTrack Ant Nav and light-sensitive rotator dial will guarantee the maximum focused sunlight onto their pitiful insect targets. Then he laughs like this: "Muhahahahahahaah!" Read More

HackersDIY
making stuff that does stuff out of stuff

| Mint | Strawberry | Plum | Peach | Blueberry | Off |

Make Your Own... Medical Stuff
We're not all about making gadgets and fusion reactors. There are all kinds of biological things you can hack together

Nicotine Patches
Man you know how hard it is to come off the nic. And you know how expensive those patches are. Well, not anymore.

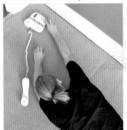

Old Soak
Soak twenty cigarettes in vodka solution for 12 days (shake every 2).

Plastered
Grab a handful of plasters. Generic 'cut knee' variants work good.

Soak & Slap
Soak the plasters in the solution and then apply topically to your ass.

Call An Ambulance
Dial for an emergency doctor as a hideous shamanic death looms

Herbal Ciagra
Sheesh. You order a load off the web. Light some candles. Fire up the old consensual partner. And... flop. Not anymore...

Fabled Wood
Source some Amazonian mimosa bark which contains many exotic chemicals.

Shaved and ready
Cut the wood into two horizontal splints not dissimilar to lollypop sticks.

Strap On
Use scotch tape to attach the splints to either side of your manhood.

You Dick
Phone an ambulance as this lame idea causes nightmarish injuries for all.

Botox
Wrinkles are so twentieth century, though smoothing worry lines is not cheap. Unless...

Visit Amazon
Take a cheap flight to the fabled South American rainforest.

Toadily Cool Man
Find a Bufo Epalpebratus toad in the jungle somewhere.

Lick It Dude Lick It
Extract the precious poisonous liquids from its pus glands without dying.

Chamen auma ambulanci!
Inject the liquid into your face while waiting for the paramedics to airlift you out.

All trademarks and registered trademarks appearing on HackersDIY.com are the property of Bahoogle.com

Net of The Living Dead

In the brief time that I've been writing these Internet Alert columns, I've seen many examples of hoaxes and fake emails around the Internet. Often they hang around long after the original has expired and you think everyone has seen them, even your wife and her annoying friend. But nope! It seems once an web con is created, it's almost impossible to stop it. And any number of gullible people will fall for it. Anyway, that's quite enough of my rambling. Here are some of most recent and persistent scams I've found lately.

Web Scammers Use New Scheme

No doubt you've seen them yourself. The 419 scam is an attempt by apparently real, often West African (or Iraqi or Phillipino - anywhere a bit far away and rubbish sounding) governmental officials to transfer huge amounts of money into your bank account. It's a scam of course. Recently, though, these scams have taken a new and compelling twist. Be alert for these new incarnations and don't you fall for them. Just below I've pasted a sample e-mail that came my way. Read it thoroughly so you don't fall it - like my bloody wife nearly did!

```
~-~-~-~-~-~-~-~-~-~-~-~-~-~-~-~-~-~-~-~-~-~-~-~-~-~-~-~-~-~-~-~-~-~-~-
Dear Sir Madam

I am Xanthar Mnar-Mnar, Chief Advisor to the Galactia Emperor Himself
Zenthaas of Planet Zorbay, from the Rigel cluster. I have recently come into
possession of 9 million igots of the purest Xanthium and need a discrete
account on your planet Earth to transfer this amount into.

I know this email must come you as a surprise, more so that we have not met
before. But it has been a long time that I have been thinking of contact
you. I have sense via metagalactic mindmeld that you are trustworthy and
GOD-fearing partner and somebody that can stand firm behind any financial
transaction and not  balk should a Carthusian Matter Ray be pointed at your
entire planet.

So please be patient to peruse and digest my proposal

A few centuries before the end of the Carthusian war, certain generals
conspired to move a large quantity of Xanthium to a secret location. My
retinal print was placed as security. Alas, the generals all met a grisly
and terrible deaths in a most systematic manner, leaving me as sole
beneficiary.

I was advised not to disclose the location and amount of Xanthium because,
well, you know what Carthusians are like. The fund is currently floating
in a space bank, concealed in an asteroid field, many parsecs from inhabited
space.  I am not allowed to own or operate an Earth account, or
indeed interact with you puny Earthlings, so I need an reputable intermediary
to act on my behalf.

For rendering this assistance, your share will be 30% of the total sum
after transfer while I will be entitled to 60% for me. Of the remainder,
7% will offset both local and intergalactic expenses that would be incurred
in the course of this transaction. The remaining 3% will be donated to the
orphans and brain-wiped zombie slaves of the Carthusian 1000 Millenium War.

"With warm hearts I offer my friendship, and my greetings, and the lengthy
insertion of my wettest Ganga Probe - and I hope this letter meets you in
good time.

yours sincerely
Xanthar

p.s. forgive my terribe spelling but despite my species having developed warp
drives, we are unable to create a decent spell check
~-~-~-~-~-~-~-~-~-~-~-~-~-~-~-~-~-~-~-~-~-~-~-~-~-~-~-~-~-~-~-~-~-~-~-
```

Book? CD? Film? 4 words 4 letters? Oo oo I know Newspaper No. Map! Oh fuck knows Letter No idea

Terrorist Bomb Making Recipe

This has been circulating around the Net for a while. You may remember the headlines. "Extremist Nuclear Bomb-Making Websites Proves We Are Right To Be Scared Of All Terrorists" and "VIRAL TERRORIST INTERNET A-BOMB THREAT TRIGGERS THIRD WORLD WAR". Here's the original email below:

Then, in a story that was less well reported, somebody actually bothered to translate the text on the page:

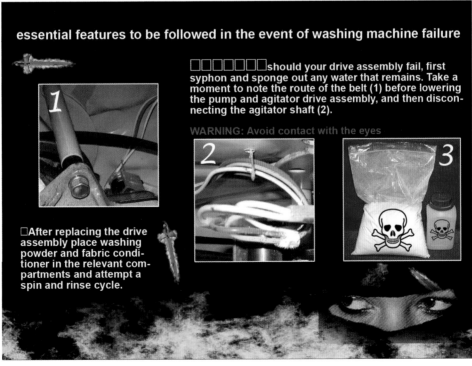

New Spam Technique

Those cursed spam writers never cease in their innovation. Their latest tactic? Reverse psychology. Either that or the entire world has gone queer.

!	□	✉	▽	⌀	From	Subject	Received ▽	Size
✉					Pet Hamm	decrease sex drive to new levels	**Fri 16/03/2007 18:10**	**117 KB**
	📨				President Bowta	Would you like to look and feel 10-20 years older?	Fri 16/03/2007 17:37	2 KB
✉					zmjruqhrh@mail.com	**Get into debt**	**Fri 16/03/2007 16:16**	**3 KB**
	📨				BittyBittyChangChang	Get 12 CDs for the price of 13!	Fri 16/03/2007 13:13	2 KB
	📨				Yiemma	Enlarge Your Penis Dangerously: 0% guranteed	Fri 16/03/2007 12:19	7 KB
	📨				KJ888	Want to lose money?	Fri 16/03/2007 10:35	1 KB
	📨				Philosopher P. Shetland	Imagine life with bills...	Fri 16/03/2007 10:28	18 KB
	📨				The Black Flipflop	Look and Feel BAD With This Complicated Hair Solution	Fri 16/03/2007 06:14	66 KB
	📨				Matchwatch	Clothed girls disinterested in your attention	Fri 16/03/2007 06:00	68 KB
✉					Freiends4uandme	**XXX Cold Dry OAPs**	Fri 16/03/2007 05:21	159 KB
✉					Hotmail Member	**Action required: your account is too empty**	Thu 15/03/2007 18:03	18 KB
	📨				SlaverBonk	Speed up your biological clock	Thu 15/03/2007 16:15	72 KB
	📨				Guiltiness S Pillbox	Replica watches - 25% more expensive than real ones	Thu 15/03/2007 13:09	2 KB
✉					Piazo	**Repulse any woman now!**	**Thu 15/03/2007 13:06**	**4 KB**

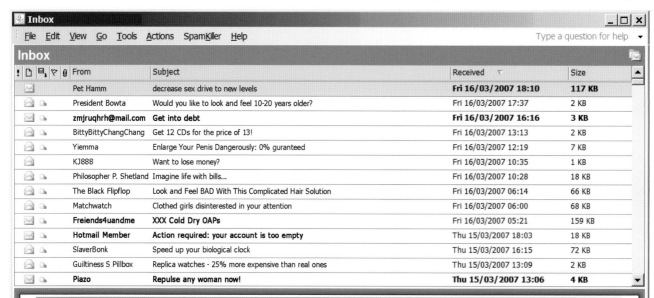

HUNG LIKE A DINOSAUR?
WOMAN ALL OVER YOU?
FRIENDS CALLING YOU 'THE TRIPOD' BEHIND YOUR BACK?
WELL WORRY NO LONGER BECAUSE

YOU TOO CAN HAVE A SMALL PENIS

- GUARANTEED NON-FDA APPROVED TREATMENT -

The same type of research that created **Ciagra** and **methamphetamine** has now created a revolutionary herbal pill that can decrease the penis by 27% in just a few short weeks.

- DECREASE LENGTH AND WIDTH
- INCREASES BLOOD PRESSURE
- RAISES CHOLESTEROL
- HAMPERS YOUR ABILITY IN BED
- MADE IN EASTERN EUROPE
- MANY NEGATIVE SIDE EFFECTS

CLICK HERE TO TRIGGER SOME POP UP ADS ▶114

Simply try these amazing pills for 30 days. If you're not 100% substantially shrunken and flaccid like an old balloon dangling on the gate of a house which hosted a children's party three days before - we'll give you more pills COMPLETELY FREE!

2870 Items

407 This page only available online

The page you are looking can be found only in our electronic edition at
http://www.theinternetnowinhandybookform.com. Cheap huh? To
incentivize you though it was probably some **hot adult content**,
probablysome gambolling Czech teens or stills from Hassel Davidoff's
famous red carpet cock slip. Why don't you quickly pop on there now
and have a look? That's it. No one's looking.

Please try one of the following:

- Close the book, wait for five seconds, then reopen it again.
- Open the Internet The Book homepage 〔◀008〕 and then look for links
  to the information you want.
- Turn ⇐ Back to the previous page and then reopen this page
  once more.

PTTP 407 - Page only available online

DIY Web 2.0 site

It's easy to make your own cutting-edge, new-paradigm, next-big-thing website. Just grab a pair of scissors and we'll show you how...

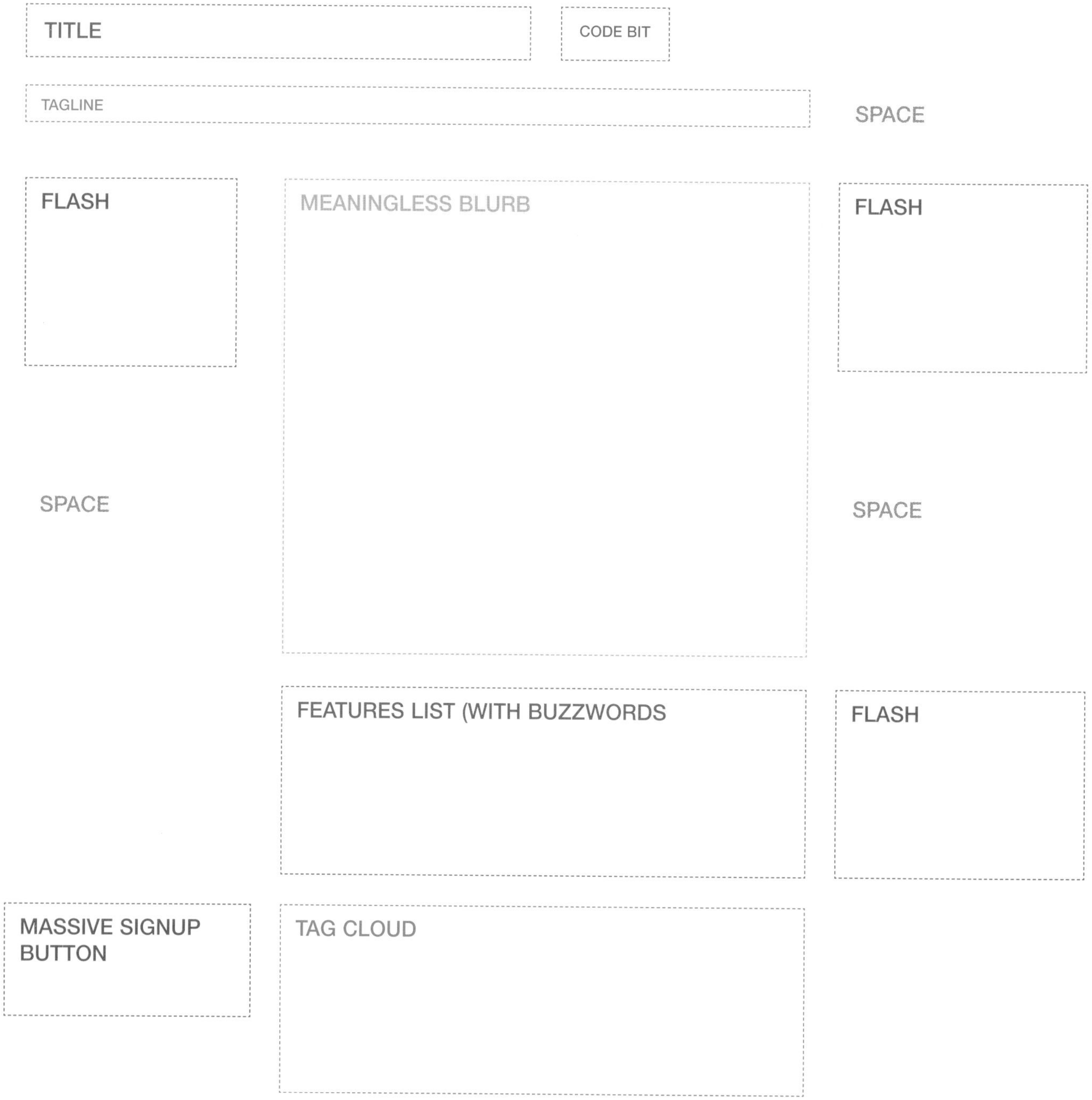

TITLE

CODE BIT

TAGLINE

SPACE

FLASH

MEANINGLESS BLURB

FLASH

SPACE

SPACE

FEATURES LIST (WITH BUZZWORDS

FLASH

MASSIVE SIGNUP BUTTON

TAG CLOUD

What is web 2.0? We've got no idea. Apparently it's good though, so best just sushhhhhhhhhh and nod your head. If you've always had a pie-in-the-sky idea that the Bahoogle corporation will definitely want to buy off you, quickly build a top of the range Web 2.0 out of these elements...

CHOOSE FROM THE OPTIONS BELOW:

SITE NAME

Take the first syllable of your first pet's name and then add one of these suffixes:

-aliser	-orama
-amundo	-mania
-arama	-ness
-arati	-plasm
-atronic	-rati
-ba	-scatter
-bix	-scopic
-bo	-ship
-bra	-ster
-city	-tabulous
-dex	-tasm
-dax	-tastic
-ee	-tion
-eo	-tits
-gasm	-tor
-gator	-town
-issimo	-tron
-losity	-ville
-lounge	-world
-o	-x
-ola	-zilla
-omi	-zo

Visit the web 2.0 name generator

UPBEAT MEANINGLESS BLURB

[name] is a Web 2.0 website developed to put you in the driving seat of the online community. With [name] can enhance your user experience, share and interact with others around the world - even more than you already do. All this through just one accessible one-stop upfront networking portal with sophisticated tagging to create a folksonomy of user feedback.

When complete, [name] will do all of the following:

BUZZ WORDS & PHRASES

(if in doubt combine several i.e. inline podcast AJAX favicons)

- import feeds
- integrate seamlessly
- inline AJAX
- Python - Anaconda - Bushmaster
- meta - micro
- mash-ups
- cascading style sheets
- blogline / blogroll
- BHTML
- tags
- user tagging
- less is more, more or less
- startup
- favicon
- export to dis.gusti.ng
- bahoogle maps API
- web 3.0
- "architecture of participation"
- Narcorati
- Picktr
- Nitro
- Long Tail
- Slashdot / Digg
- Zodcasting
- folksomy
- user-based experience
- AJAX
- a joke about AJAX - you know good for blocked drains etc
- folksomy (again)

TAGCLOUD

A tagcloud is a clump of the most popular subjects on a site or, in this example, unpopular subjects. The bigger the font size, the more people who agree.

most unpopular tags on the Internet today

altruism believing that all your parents need is MDMA and that'll change them forever bronski beat brotherhood of man brussel sprouts docking death by barbeque fondue (especially cheese) grandma's folds god landlines mucrosoft neun and neunzig luftballoon people who manifest the secret reading books self restraint shutting down the laptop and going out for a nice walk the word 'dudebox' technicolour dreamcoats tinpot Korean iZod clones web3.0 washing your pernieum work working warez installer themes

THE**TRUTH**THE**TRUTH**THE**TRUTH**.COM

Cutting through the media-fed cover-up on aliens, 11/9, robots, crop circles, Area 52, pole-reversal and the coming dawning of the Christ Consciousness in 2012.

Home	Archive	Shop	Store	Web Design

Headlines

- **11/9 The Zionist Shape-Shifting Satan Aliens Did It**
- **Obesity Epidemic - Harvest Plan For Space Lizards**
- **Huge Towel Found Inside The Earth**
- **Marijuana - Damn This Shit's Good**
- **Male Impotence Epidemic Linked To Alien Oestrogen Chemicals In The Water Not To Lack Of General Robustness As My Girlfriend Unceasingly Claims**

DON'T TAKE MY WORD FOR IT
Take some magic mushrooms (or cannabis that's quite good too) and you'll see that Gaia is birthing a neo-cortex in the shape of the internet. We are nerve-endings in this new brain part and we will soon realise this and love will conquer all.

Life on Mars? Yesssssss

If Anyone wants true proof that there was and "is" life on mars - including forests, rivers, shopping malls, sluices, breathable atmospheres, football teams, remains of pyramids, tombolas, even crashed intergalactic space vessels with lasers and everything - watch this film on YouFlue and pass on the information. Don't ever forget: Nassa are full of shit. And their masters the PENTACON. There is a massive cover-up like the assassination of Princess Dido and the real faked moon landings, capricorn 1 and the J-Lo Simpson landings. And The Earth is flat not round like the scientists say. MARS HAD AN ADVANCED HUMANOID CIVILISARTION THAT WAS DESTROYED IN A SOLAR SYSTEM WIDE WAR THAT RIPPED MARS APART. THE RACE WAS KNOWN AS THE CARTHUSIANS AND THEY SETTLED IN THE MIDDLE EAST AND IN AREAS OF CENTRAL AFRICA. IF YOU HAVE A PROBLEM AND NO ONE ELSE CAN HELP, AND IF YOU CAN FIND THEM, MAYBE THEY CAN HELP YOU.
THE QUESTION IS WHY THE COVER-UP??? I HAVE RACKED MY BRAINS AND CANNOT WORK OUT WHY THESE PEOPLES ARE SPENDING SO MUCH TIME AND EFFORT COVERING UP THE TRUTH.
The Governments of the entire whole world perpetuate these cover-ups and then they peddle this racist Darwinina Evolution bullshit. It's obnvious that we are decended from angelic space aliens who visited our planet thousands of years ago in golden robes. As usual we are being massively deceived and human unconsciousness is finally waking up into the divien light of christ consciousness in 20212, the reveasal of the poles, the return of The Maya, and the reapperance of Champion The Wonderhorse to our televisions.
KIND REGARDS
PETER.

Mysterious Nebula Final Proof That The Heavens Are Full Of Signs

Nassa, when not carrying out cover-up after cover-up to hide the truth of alien life all around us, have photographed an unprecendented "double penetration" nebula near the centre of our galaxy. This is clearly a passageway to another dimension and probably the route which the many mysterious cigar-shaped objects are coming from on a daily basis.

HISTORY REWRITTEN? YOU BET

As we all know very strong evidence is emerging that the years 1815-1915 have been completely made-up. How else do you account for the sudden leap in human development? This century was inserted into history by the shape-shifting illuminati to conver up the sudden acquisition of alien technologies including stargates, mind wipers like in Men In Black and lasers (not like the Star War ones. More like in Blake 7. Those).

This Year's Crop Of Cropcircles from England, UK

THE CROP CIRCLES SHOWN HERE ARE SOME OF THE MOST INTRIGUING TO COME INTO PUBLIC KNOWLEDGE FOR MANY YEARS. MANY OBSERVERS BELIEVE THESE ARE HERALDING A NEW PLAYFUL PHASE OF CROP CIRCLE ACTIVITY. THE "EARTHLY" MESSAGES SUGGESTING THAT THE ALIENS ARE ALREADY PREPARING TO COME DOWN TO EARTH AHEAD OF THE DAWNING OF THE CHRIST CONSCIOUSNESS AND WORLD PEACE IN 2012

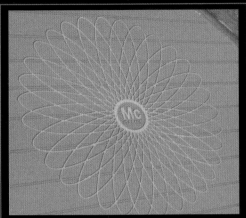

Wayland Linky Bit, near Ashenbourne
A dazzling 'spiroglyph' one of many seen the area, in different coloured fields, some overlapping pointlessly. Again a 'playful' motif.

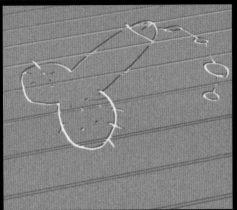
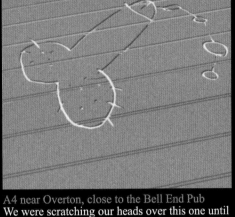

A4 near Overton, close to the Bell End Pub
We were scratching our heads over this one until veteran crop circle expert Danziel Penderback pointed out it was a huge cock and balls.

Pirate's Cove, Dorset
An intriguing formation showing evidence of knowledge of advanced theorems, harmonic ratios, and the best way to source 0 day warez. We detected a small amount of damage is consistent with a three handed (or three tentacled) extra terrestrial who use base 3 for all their communications.

Goat Farm, Bottomwell
Excited about this one until Danziel showed me the website. Bloody dirty alien bastards.

In my backgarden
The wheat was pressed down extremely flat on this one. No way a human could've done that.

109

The Worst Restaurants 6 photos / 0 views

Sets | Tags | Archives | Favorites | Popular | Profile

Ring Road, Basingerstoke

High Street, Chippingbournesodbury

Stoke McNewington, London

Peckingham Lane, Chelm

Little Ham, Ham On Rye

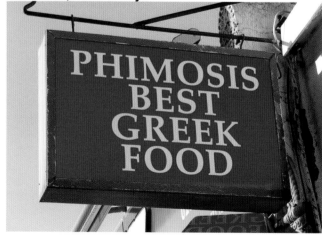

Liver St, London

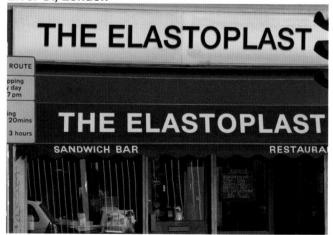

The Meme Museum

archiving popular web phenomenon for future generations

Get Your War On

Tuesday 16th March

The response to my informal Sunday-only posts from your hobbies series has been positive. A number of you have submitted stories and questions. I'll do my best to say etc and a lot do you remember

And a snippet from the less well-known 'GET YOUR UNDERWEAR ON' - an ill-coinceived mash-up of a tabloid newspapers sex advice cartoon and the famed satirical strip.

DiggIt This • Save To Dis.Gusti.Ng • 0 comments.

Fat Chick In Party Hats

Monday 15th March

This infamous website was very popular in the politically uncorrect 20th century. Less well known are the myriad of spin-offs sites that tried to ride the obesity bandwagon.
Slim Blokes In Funeral Hats
Fat Chicks In Party Scat (NSFW)
Fat Chicks In Party Chaps (NSFW)
Fat Chicks Breaded As Goujons

DiggIt This • Save To Dis.Gusti.Ng • 0 comments.

Squillion Dollar Page

Sunday 14th March

Clever but poor anthropology student Marcus Langstrat was down on his luck and dollars while studying at university. Facing a huge rent bill, his choices were: either a fortnight down the docks. Or some hair-brained scheme involving the internet. He plumped for the latter. He came up with the idea to sell pixels on his webpage for a dollar each to an audience of low-brow, craze-chasing stupidos. It worked. Within weeks, Langstrat had raised over $48 million dollars, enough to buy his own docks and help other poor students to work the cobblestoned back alleys in safety with regular health checks while he lorded it over the oceans in a huge yacht staffed entirely by nude Natashas.

Digg This • Save To Dis.Gusti.Ng • 0 comments.

Explosive Emails

Sunday 14th March

The political power of the email.

COMMENTS

Johnathon says: "There are several misalignments on this page. "

Darren says: "Want some pictures of my wife to circulate as memes? You could do a joke about how jilted ex-partners are always uploading pictures of their spouses online or something. That would be funny"

Wikipedant says: "You must let me point out that there are several misalignments on this page. Also its ONLY BTML 2.3 version compliant. Amateurs! I for one won't be signing up to newsletter. It probably still using the Onyx Beta. "

Sophia says: "Hi! I'm Sophia from Arabia. I'm looking for pretty gays and guys to pratise my French on."

KeepItLight says: "Is it me or is this page not particularly entertaining. Most of the best 'memes' are missing. What about Mahir or that fat Zardoz kid for example?"

The Meme Museum
archiving popular web phenomenon for future generations

Hat Or Not?
Sunday 14th March

Who can forget this classic?

Am I Wearing a HAT or NOT ?

Please select a rating to see the next picture.

○ 0   ○ 1

NOT ▬▬▬▬▬▬▬▬▬▬▬▬▬▬▬▬▬▬ HAT

Are you wearing a hat?
Submit your picture and find out!

User Login	
Username	
Password	
	Login

STOP!

You are about to enter The DarkNet.

There the pages are black and the typography is LARGE and LURID.
The following pages are protected by PageTurnPass, a premiere security system.
You must prove your age before you can access the PREMIUM CONTENT beyond.

Answer the following questions as truthfully as possible.
Then check your score at the bottom of the page.

MULTIPLE CHOICE ROUND 1

1. What do you do on Friday nights?
a) Knit
b) Stay in and prepare a delicious salade nicoise. Oo yum!
c) Go out, cause mayhem and end up in bed with your best friends
d) Go to bed and dream of driving a big red tractor

2. What is Kajagoogoo?
a) Pardon?
b) An outmoded musical act
c) A great new web 2.0 startup that does something way cool
d) A funny jumping animal with a wobbly tail

3. What percentage of your income goes towards your pension?
a) I am drawing my pension
b) 20%
c) 0%
d) I only get £1.50 pocket money every Friday

4. Your parents are...?
a) dead
b) my friends
c) my enemies
d) my mummy and daddy

5. What is your greatest fear?
a) no one posts a comment on your mineminemyspace page for 2 days
b) Alzheimers
c) AIDS
d) the dark

BONUS ROUND

6. Do you own a tea cosy?

7. Do you have a laminated corporate ID?

8. Do you know what's currently Number 1 in the charts?

9. Do you like a nice beaker of sugar water kiddo?

PICTURE ROUND

10. Is this where you live?

11. Is this where you dreamed you would live?

12. Is this where you want to live?

MULTIPLE CHOICE ROUND 2

13. How many crumpled, yellowing boxes of exotic herbal teas do you have languishing untouched at the back of your kitchen cupboard?
a) I can't reach the back of the kitchen cupboard
b) over 5
c) none
d) 1

14. Pssst! Do you want some of these here drugs?
a) I hereby perform a citizen's arrest
b) Sound. I'm in
c) No thanks, I have to get up tomorrow and mow the lawn
d) Will they make me feel funny?

15. When was the last time you had sex with your partner?
a) 1988
b) Three weeks ago
c) Yesterday
d) Hahaha, you said "sex"

16. Do you fancy having an affair?
a) Oh... not really, I'm reading the paper right now
b) Uh, whatever
c) Stop touching me or I'll call the police
d) Oh yes please, that sounds titillating, mysterious, forbidden and emotionally exhilerating

QUICK FIRE ROUND

17. Have you ever...?
a)...contemplated suicide?
b)...committed suicide?
c)...started smoking?
d)...given up smoking?
e)...worried about your back?
f)...felt self-conscious in a bar?
g)...said 'this has got a good beat'?
h)...weighed yourself and sighed?
i)...slept with your best friends' partner?
j)...repeatedly?
k)...simultaneously?
l)...and blogged about it?
m)...used an artifical sweetner?

ANSWERS

Add up your scores to reveal your age.
1 a=3 b=2 c=1 d=0; 2 a=2 b=2 c=1 d=0; 3 a=4 b=2 c=1 d=0; 4 a=3 b=2 c=1 d=0; 5 a=1 b=3 c=2 d=0; 6 yes=3, no=1; 7 yes=2 no=1; 8 yes=2 no=0; 9 yes=3 no=1; 10 yes=1 no=0; 11 yes=2 no=1; 12 yes=3 no=0; 13 a=0 b=2 c=1 d=2; 14 a=4 b=1 c=2 d=1; 15 a=3 b=2 c=1 d=0; 16 a=3 b=1 c=0 d=1
Quick Fire round - if you answered yes, add or subtract the following scores:
a +2; b +5; c +1; d +1;e +2; f +2; g +5; h +2; i + 1; j +2; k +3; l -5; m +4

IF YOU SCORED MORE THAN 21
YOU MAY TURN THE PAGE [▶131]

PornForGirlsByGirls.com ™

HOME PAGE | **NO MEMBERS** | **GIRL-OFF-GIRL** | **FOREPLAY** | **FOREPLAY** | **FOREPLAY**

EXTREME
CONSIDERATION

These pretty boys know exactly how to support you!

HUGE WET
SMILING EYES

JOIN NOW* AND GET INSTANT ACCESS TO 500,000 PICS
* After careful weighing up of the alternatives and a couple of lengthy chats with a few of your closest friends

of hand written love letters

HARDCORE
SOCIABLE LUNCH WITH THE PARENTS

MULTIPLE GIFTS
wave after wave of shiny presents!

`spacer.gif`

BAD BOYS
TURNED GOOD

ROUGHLY TAKEN
on a chocolate weekend to Belgium

pearl necklaces
Tahitian Southsea

only £59

WATCH OUR FREE VIDEO CLIPS

WEDDING DRESS

20 Minute clip of a single button on a bursting wedding dress being slowly unpicked on a windy moor. At dawn. Near some trees.

"ARMS"

Close-up of a pair of big veiny arms, stained in oil, fixing a motorcycle. And a group of shirtless tree surgeons scaling an old pine.

"FINGERS"

Watch this two hour video of a topless finger massage. Each finger delicately and pain-stakingly oiled and rubbed and kissed.

"LONG SEXY STRIP"

Watch extreme close-ups of the floorboards and skirting being stripped by your boyfriend while you lie on the sofa drinking hot chcocolate.

REAL GUY
The incredible latex boyfriend.

NOW talks in a deep baritone voice

"Porn? What's that?"
"My female friends? They're all ugly"

"Here - have all my passwords!"
"And you can read my emails and texts"

MEMBERS | SUPPORT | CARING | LOVING | TENDERNESS
Check out our sister sites! Nape Fantasies and of course: XXX Hardcore Inaction

Broadsheet tests new handy supplement

First Music, then Yoga, then Eating, then ... grot?

London broadsheet *The Preserver* has upped the stakes in the Sunday newspaper wars,
if these leaked proofs of their new monthly magazine are to be believed. Maybe the
newspaper - read primarily by middle class people in spectacles around a Gastropub
table with braying friends - is about to nail a new daring segment in the marketplace?

The Preserver
PORN
MAGAZINE

CONTENTS NOVEMBER2008

Girl-on-Girl
62

10
80s porn

14
Sex Tape

CONTRIBUTORS

Edwin Lacter
Guest-reviewer Lacter has done it all: on and off camera, two handed, one handed, fist, noose and fancy, under desk, online and in-flight.

Tarquin Chormdeley-Bass
Renown wanker and raconteur visits Kenya and Sierra Leone to report on a new form of porn that could save Africa from disintegration.

NEXT MONTH

DON'T MISS
In the next issue of The Preserver Porn Monthly out on 10th December: Porn Of The Dead: How Necro is Back Back Black.

ON THE COVER

Chantele and Suzie warm up back stage

402 Payment Required

The page you are looking can be found in our premium paid-for content area. If you want in, you're going to have to pay. Oh yeah. Visit the online-edition of the book at http://www.theinternetnowinhandybookform.com and pay a subscription fee. We'll send you a password. Thank you!

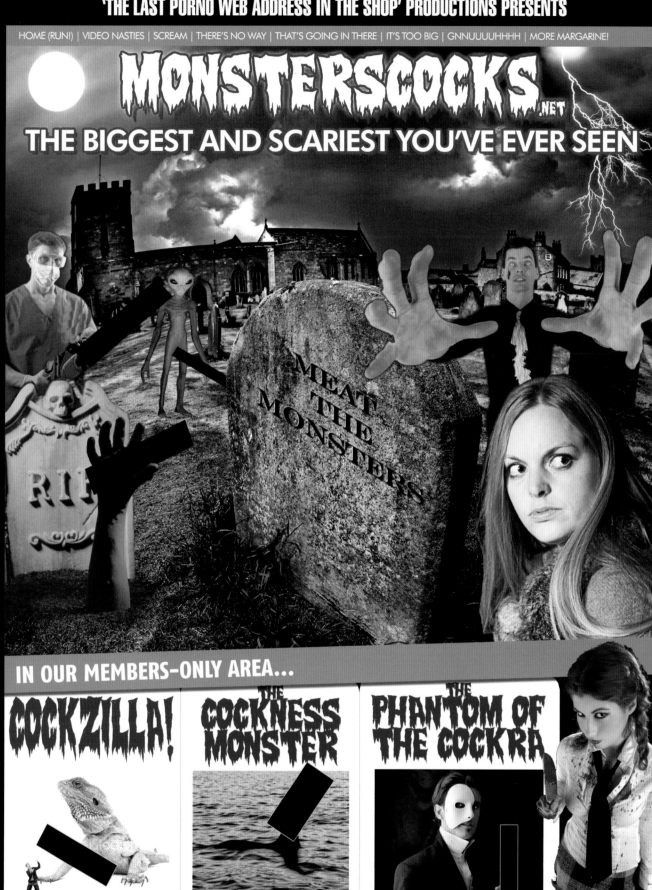

you triggered some unsexy pop-up ads

YOU CAN FLICK
BUT YOU
CAN'T HIDE

There are pages that provide legal reads. This is not one of them.

This piece of paper has been permanently wiped by court order because it facilitated the free viewing of copyrighted images and text. And words. And badly scanned segments from ebooks on Nostradamus prophecies and other geeky subjects. And really off-the-wall Jap Anime. All kinds of stuff. It was a real conceptual mess.

(Man, some of the stuff was crazy. There was one where this chick was shooting lasers out of her - well you gotta see it. Rob from Investigation's got it at home. Along with a bunch of stuff from previous busts. Too much!)

Illegal 'free-reading' such materials in 'books' such as these 'over someone's shoulder' or 'borrowing from a library' violates the law. Which law, we're not sure, but think about it. How can stuff be free? How would that work?

The current epidemic of 'free reading' is robbing thousands of honest, hard-working capitalists of their holiday homes. It's also stifling creativity, bombing children, upsetting our wives and our politicians. It's also against God, in case you were wondering, and may even be a contributing factor to colon cancer and type II diabetes.

It's also theft. You could get caught and be sent to prison.

Do you want to go to prison? Have you not read the *Shawshaft Redemption.Scanned.pdf FFS*? That's what prison's really like. Wall-to-wall anal rape and beatings. Sometimes both at the same time.
(I know because Rob from Investigations has the pics to prove it.)

So remember Shawshaft. Your ass is on the line.

PAAP
THE PAPER ASSOCIATION OF AMERICA POLICE

406 This page nixed by the lawyers

The page you are looking at has been no-no'ed by the lawyers. Those spineless, wig-wearing judge lickers. Damn, it was a good page. One of the best. But thanks to deeply restrictive libel laws in the UK, the jokes were considered too risky for general consumption.

Please try one of the following:

- Close the book, wait for five seconds, then reopen it again.
- Visit http://www.theinternetnowinhandybookform.com and see if we haven't managed to sneak the page online somewhere.
- Sssssshhhhhhhhhh!

PTTP 406 - Page Nixed By Lawyers

409 The dog ate this page, honest miss

Sorry. And then, right, and then Hammer Davis stole my bag, miss, and gobbed on it and threw it on the roof. And it had my pottery homework in it and my eggs for home economics, miss.

Please try one of the following:

- Give the snivelling little brat detention and extra work.
- Take pity on the poor child. He's obviously telling the truth.
- Give it some Ritalin. That'll shut it up.

PTTP 409 - Dog ate page

 # Narcorati
Who's taking what. Right now.

Hide [_____] in the cistern ▾ [Hide] Advanced hide

About Us

Drugs. Drugs. Drugs. That's what we're about. They're just a normal part of human experience. Mankind has been getting into altered states since, like, the beginning of all of time. And perhaps even before that. We celebrate and aggregate all drug activity on the web. Enjoy!

Popular

2012 - The Return Of My Sanity
a new book by Danziel Penderback
"I, a cynical journalist looking for meaning, read loads of books about Mayan prophecies of the end of the world in 2012, the evolution of consciousness, and crop circles. I then took loads of psychedelic drugs and had a prophetic vision of the evolution of consciousness coming in 2012 and crop circles signalling that end to me, a former cynical journalist. It was very meaningful. "Good" *Rolling Stoned.* "Bobbins." *Everyone else*

Article

Do It Yourself Drugs How to simulate the effects of illegal substances with legal substances

 Amphetamines Drink 5 cans of Redbull, smoke 15 cigarettes and drink 3 cups of coffee as fast as you can (every two to three minutes is good!)

 Cannabis Take 20 Nytols with around 6 beers. Rub vinegar in your eyes. Sustain a minor head injury. Oh and don't eat for two days

 Heroin Submerge yourself in a hot bubble bath, while eating 2 tubs of Ben & Jerry's, and receiving a massage from a loving partner. Round off with six immodiums.

 Ecstasy Lock yourself in a dark veal crate for a month and then burst out at a party.

 Cocaine Go around in a little gang. Visit the toilet every 20 minutes. Talk uproariously about yourself. Stay up 'til 4am. Have sex but under no circumstances climax.

 LSD Meditate, in a fetal position, for six weeks. Then buy a selection of random multi-coloured lizards and snakes and beetles and let them out in your room.

 Crack Train for 10 years as an astronaut. Qualify for a journey on the space shuttle. Strap yourself in. Listen to the countdown. 3 ... 2 ... 1 ... Blast off! Crash land 10 minutes later.

 Comedown Put your head in a vice. Listen to Slint. C'est tout.

New

The latest top drawer weed from Holland

Choccy's Orange Scuff   Tarmac   Kushtea   Lung Treacle   Semtex Royal Cream   Pecan Double Nut Haze   More...

Shop

Music

featuring: 9 to 5, Men At Work, Please Please Please Let Me Get Some Sleep

GAKNAV
· portable, lightweight wallet-sized cocaine locator
· dual-use mirrored screen
· satellite technology to locate cocaine of all types: Bolivian, Columbian and baby milk powder

Trip Hamper
Psychedelicacies include: a conch to stroke, citrus fruit, mirror (wrapped), candles, a poster of some fractals and chlorapromazine in case it goes a bit *Jacob's Ladder*

Psychonaut's Birthday?
With built-in Autechre / Ulrich Schnauss / Koyaanisqatsi playback, ATM is the only guaranteed way to neutralise 'bad energy' before getting into the local paper with your trippy exploits

Nose Job
For when your septum collapses, a deluxe bionic Nose made from the highest grade brushed titanium.

 **the best-selling rolling papers**
We Have No Idea What These Are Used For. Honest. Big Cigarettes? See? Clueless. Bye!

Narcorati

Who's taking what. Right now.

Hide [_____] [in the cistern ▼] [Hide] Advanced hide

When drugs are legal how will they be marketed?

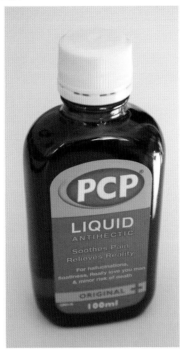

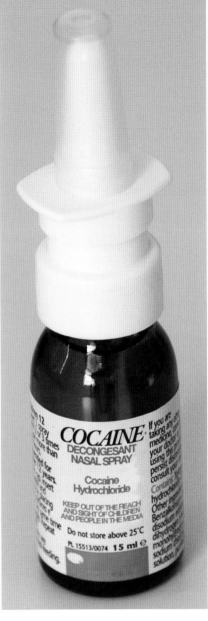

modern adventure days.com
give your loved one a short-lived experience they'll never forget

HOME   HOW LIFE WORKS   BIRTH   A STRING OF EXPERIENCES   CONFUSION   DEATH

CATEGORIES
- LOVE
- DRIVING FAST BRIEFLY
- FLEETING ADVENTURE
- HUMILIATION
- LOSS
- DEPRESSION
- RECOVERY
- WEALTH
- FAME
- HEALTH
- JOY
- FREEDOM

SPECIALS
- ★ GOLD
- ★ PLATINUM
- ★ TITANIUM
- ★ SEABORGIUM
- ★ MENDELEVIUM
- ★ EXCELLENTIUM

MOST POPULAR

FOR HIM

1 Be A Russian MP
2 Instore DJ
3 Deliverance 4 A Day
4 Autistic Savant
5 Starlet's Bodyguard
(fake danger)

FOR HER

1 Chocolate
2 Pampering
3 Chocolate
4 Pampering
5 Chocolate Pampering

one for the girls...

*Vampyre Queen for a day**

*night

features:
- stay in 5 star castle dungeon
- hot tub of purest virginal blood
- pampering by lesbian courtesans
- luxury silk-lined coffin
- no reflection in the mirror!

Unforgettable gift experiences

We have hundreds of unforgettable, shocking, appalling, often debauched adventure days for you to savour. From exotic violent fantasies to saturating spa days through to death-defying stunts for those too desensitised to feel anything anymore, there's a gift for for every person, every occasion. Experience the heights of modern human experience **today**.

And one for the boys...

We stick you up a mountain with a sizeable portion of your brain removed. See if you can crawl down to basecamp using just your teeth. Betcha can't! Yeah that's a challenge.

Most popular this week

Psychedelic Guru
Burning Man! Heiresses! Hieresses! Burning Man!

Death Of Your Mother
Centre stage on the most grief-stricken day of your life (in a nice little black number)

Pinochet For A Day
Consolidate power with death squads. Embezzle with impunity. Then die.

It comes in a box

To make your experience more tangible and less transient, each Experience Day comes in a beautiful red box with sections and flaps and a big bow (for women) or in a grubby brown parcel hidden behind a urinal which then self-destructs (for men). **Learn more**

Corporate Solutions	**Testimonials**	**For Couples**	**Testimonials**
Hey bossman! Our Group Experience Days can help your team better pretend that they're a team of people who like each other.	"We all went Paintballing for the day. It's amazing what a few welts and day wearing a mask in shitty forest can do for morale!"	Reinvigorate your stale love or just get turned on doing something weird and a bit dirty. We have handfuls of Couples Days to row over.	"Sharon and I chose 'Romans For A Day'. Burning Christians was fun (as ever!) but the vomitorium? Sharon wasn't so sure."
more	more	more	more

modern adventure days.com
give your loved one a short-lived experience they'll never forget

HOME   HOW LIFE WORKS   BIRTH   A STRING OF EXPERIENCES   CONFUSION   DEATH

CATEGORIES
LOVE
DRIVING FAST BRIEFLY
FLEETING ADVENTURE
HUMILIATION
LOSS
DEPRESSION
RECOVERY
WEALTH
FAME
HEALTH
JOY
FREEDOM

TOP SELLERS

Choose one of our hot sellers if you want to know what it feels like to be free. Free from money stresses. Free from responsibility. Free to act in any way you want. Free. Free. Free! Prices start at just £11.99.

FILTER RESULTS   Price (any) ⌄   Location (any) ⌄   **REFINE**

Name	Location	Price

Evil Master Mind Whisked away to an island hideaway, you'll be kitted out with a fluffy cat, toothy henchman and a big, red self-destruct button. Also on hand is wavering double agent Clitoria Lickwell and personal secretary Miss FlangeYummy who will gladly take your... **more**   £14,000, 000,000, 000,000, 000   ADD

Asylum Seeker Experience the generosity of advanced Western culture first hand. Doubted right from the start, you'll be herded into a laid-back holding camp. There you'll be subjected to various interviews before being shipped back from whence you came. **more**   £15,000   ADD

Olden Days Be transported back to the days before crime, sex pests, health scares and the internet. Leave your doors unlocked. Let your naked children play with 'Uncle Harry'. Eat whatever you want (6 sugars in your tea, lard on toast). Feel a real sense of community. And then die of a mild bacterial infection. **more**   2d, 1s   ADD

Media Scapegoat We're not racist. Who can be? That's right. You are! Feel the full force of a sudden media witch hunt as the feelings society can't accept in itself get projected wholesale onto you. Ignorance is no defence. Burn the witch! **more**   £Free   ADD

No Boundaries For A Day It's no holes barred with no repercussions. Engage in scatplay, armed robbery, and eye contact. Cross the gender boundary. Take drugs. Take part in an open-mic night. Comes with a free a teaspoon of your favourite ink cleaner. **more**   £25   ADD

Religious For A Day Everything is beautiful when you've got your own personal hotline to the almighty. Spend a day being doe-eyed and smiley yet quietly judgemental. Choose from a range of pre-packed, off the shelf ideologies. Feel safe and pure. **more**   £donation   ADD

Atheist Pious superiority. Lack of conclusive evidence for your suppositions. Preachy. Why it's just ... like being religious. Yes join the growing popular cult of "no god" and spend an angry, seething day raging at an existence devoid of meaning as far as you're able to perceive it. **more**   £11.99   ADD

Cuckold MEN ONLY. Yep, she's lost attraction for you. But you're too weak to either re-engage the relationship or duff up the opposition. And everybody knows it! This age-old form of humiliation is now yours to experience first hand. **more**   50% of your salary   ADD

このページを読んでいる日本人として、君はため息をついているに違いない（もしくは日本文化の耐え難さとアンニュイを象徴する見当違いな異文化理解に対してならなんでも）。

ため息。だってほらまた別のページで "crazy" な日本人を笑いの種にしているから。

あはは、日本人はおかしな食べ物をたべてんでしょ。
いひひ、日本のポルノは全部モザイクかかってるし。
うふふ、日本の男は女子高生でエッチな夢をみるんだと。

日本文化の微妙なニュアンスを伝えようとする無謀な試みはたいていどちらかのパターンに落ち着く。

一つは、田舎の鍛え上げられたZENの師匠が片手で盆栽を刈り込みながら、もう片方の手で自分の息子をこする‥、

それか、時代の先端をいく（と思い込んでいる）都会人がアルミホイルにくるまれながら、Hentaiタコ型ロボットたちがセックスをすることで世界をめちゃくちゃに破壊してしまうという内容の映画をみているか、どちらか。

13:30～13:40	第一印象はとにかくこんな感じ。	
13:40～14:20	でも実のところ、このページは、もっと何か唐突に別の文化に入り込んでしまったときに体験するような突然の目眩のようなものについてなんだ。	
14:20～14:50	まるでカンザス州の小屋から飛び出したら、そこはもう別の場所のような。	
14:50～15:20	そんなウェブサイトがあって、それをbrowseしているときに君は突然気づくかもしれない。すぐそこに全く別のインターネットの世界があるってことに。	
15:20～15:35	それは英語ではなくて‥、	
15:35～16:55	ちょっと自分の国のものに似ているけど、でも何かおかしい。	
16:55～17:00	ちょっとくだらない、うん。	
17:00～18:30	それでいて少しばかりダサい。	

そして今この瞬間、君はページを覗き込んで意味をつなげようとやっきになっている。

1）これは何のウェブサイトなのか？
一体全体ここで何が起きてるの？
このエロサイトは仕事場のパソコンのファイアーウォールも通り抜けちゃうわけ？

2）IT分野における巨大なポルノ産業への警鐘は鳴らされているの？
僕のIPアドレスは記録されてしまって、今まさに僕とセックスするために壁を通り抜けようとしているHentaiタコ型ロボットたちによって占拠された巨大なブラックタワーに送信されてしまったの？？

I Hope so そう願う。

THE WAR ON CLIMATE
News From The Frontline On The Global War Against Rogue Weather

PLANETARY THREAT ADVISORY LEVEL

SHITEHAUS

Explore The Site
Army
Navy
Red Indian
Construction Worker

Current Operations
Enduring Carbon
Excellent Shinyness

Current Wars
War On Plastic
War On Non Compact
Flourescent Light
Bulbs
War On Slippery
Pavement Stones

POSTERS

Download and put these up around in your neighbourhoods.

OPERATION
ENDURING CARBON

MOST-WANTED
EMISSIONS

PLEASE ENSURE THAT PRIORITIZATION OF
THE EMERGENCY CAPTURIZATION OF
THESE EMERGING GASES IS PRIORITIZED

BREAKING NEWS

ICEBERGS TO AFGHANISTAN The arctic iceshelf is displacing water causing coastal erosion to US interests around the world. A military response is called for. State of the art H60 helicopters of the Arctic Snow Dispersal Mobile Unit 3, Multi-National Division will airlift icebergs and drop them on Afghanistan where they will rapidly melt. The nation will flood, drowning opium poppy plantations and some of the population. Operation Ice Ice Baby will commence this summer. **more**

ON THE GROUND

Iran Primary Cause Of Global Warming

Recent secret research by Pentagon scientists has concluded that much of the excess heat in the world is coming from Iran, a very hot country. The scientists recommend an enforced nuclear winter to rapidly cool off the situation. The President has authorised the delivery of several multi-megaton bombs to the region. **Story.**

Algae Fields To Be Bombed

Toxic algae blooms are becoming more and more common in our oceans and lakes due to fertiliser run off and growing water temperatures. US Army Brigade Engineers have come up with an innovative solution: airstrikes. **Story**

MORE STORIES

National Guard Mobilised Across The US To Turn Off Appliances Left On Stand-By
New powers allow forced entry if little red light spotted through window or reported by honest neighbours.

Additional Fencing To Be Rolled Out All Along Our South Border With Mexico
To um, keep out possible snow drifts, sand storms and other undesirables.

Checkpoints Established On All Major Roads To Ensure Cars Are Being Shared
Unauthorized vehicles containing just one passenger and or some small children will likely be fired upon.

IN OTHER NEWS
Emission-heavy SUVs To Be Impounded At Gun Point (Hummers okay)
Three Incandescent Lights Bulbs Are You're Out

OUR LEADER SPEAKS

The President Of The United States outlines mission goals on the newly announced War On Climate

WASHINGTON Today - "Citizens of the world. We are engaged in a global struggle against a murderous enemy that despises freedom and crushes all dissent under tsunamis and the such. This climate has territorial ambitions and pursues totalitarian aims. Against such an enemy there is only one response. WAR. We have already made substantial progress in degrading the global climate network, destroying, eliminating and disrupting wherever and whenever we find climate. We will never back down. We will never give in. We will never accept anything less than complete victory."

MISSION GOALS

The aims of this important mission are fivefold

1 Defeat violent climate, a clear and present threat to our way of life

2 Prevent attacks by climate systems

3 Punish states and individuals who support climate

4 Deny climate any area it could use as a base or launching pad for shit weather

5 Create a global environment hospitable to American values and business

ENERGY INEFFICIENT NATIONS

The latest satellite data showing our enemies in the War On Climate.

Our secret data shows conclusively that Iran, North Korea, Venezuela, Afghanistan and France are the worst offenders.

Missile-based Cloud Defence | Joint Chiefs Of Nephograph
CENTCOM | FUCOM | COMEON | ROMCOM | SPAMCOM | WESTBROM | DADUMDOM

You've reached the end of The Internet Now In Handy Book Form

Congratulations! This is the last page.

Thank you for reading. There are no more pages.

You must now close the book and go do something productive.

Like checking your email. Or browsing some electronic webpages.

That's it.

Had enough?

Complete our customer experience survey and you could win an iZod!

Hey. As the vast corporate producers of The Internet: Now In Handy Book Form! we're interested in what you think. You're important to us. Your views and opinions will help us shape bigger and better strategies for milking more money from you. By knowing you, we can better target you. That's our motto.

(We know our official public motto is "Come Join Us In The Playground Of Life" but this is our secret internal motto.)

Just answer the questions below.

Out of ten, how satisfied are you with The Internet Now In Handy Book Form! in each of following categories?
- ☐ Overall Quality
- ☐ Value For Money
- ☐ Interactive Excellence
- ☐ Fingerfeel
- ☐ Learning Curve
- ☐ Toilet Read Worthiness

How long have you owned The Internet Now In Handy Book Form!?
- ☐ Not Long
- ☐ Not That Long
- ☐ That Long
- ☐ Long
- ☐ Too Long

How often do you open The Internet Now In Handy Book Form!?
- ☐ Constantly
- ☐ Regularly
- ☐ Rarely
- ☐ Barely
- ☐ What is this Handy book you keep mentioning?

Compared to other internet books that are available (WWWow, for example, or Schatt's Internetty), would you say that The Internet: Now In Handy Book Form! is...?
- ☐ Infinitely Superior
- ☐ Ahead By A Length
- ☐ Completely Identical
- ☐ Found To Be Wanting
- ☐ A Pale Imitation

How likely are you to recommend The Internet Now In Handy Book Form to friends?
- ☐ I've Bought 20 Copies To Distribute Amongst Them in a slightly evangelical fashion
- ☐ I'll Probably Introduce It Into Conversation
- ☐ I'm Not Going To Mention It
- ☐ I'll Make A Point Of Saying It's Rubbish
- ☐ I'll Warn Against It At All Costs

What would you like to tell the Bahoogle Corporation about your satisfaction with The Internet: Now In Handy Book Form! that has not been expressed in this survey?

Finally please add your email address and postal address.
*All addresses will be added to an insecure off-shore database and will be used to target you with junk for the rest of your life.

_____

_____

_____

_____

Tech Support

If you're having trouble using PageTurn™ technology, or just experiencing difficulty reading or understanding the subtle interplay of satire and nob jokes, you've come to the right place. Our trained support staff are available 24/7. Yes, 24 days a year, 7 years every century, our friendly tech support people will be happy to help you.

KNOWN TECHNICAL ISSUES

Visual Hardware
The visuals in this book are compatible only with Eyes version 6.3 and above. If you cannot see a spinning globe with the universe exploding in the background somewhere on this page, you may need to upgrade your eyes to get the full experience.

Copy Protection
This book is fitted with the latest digital rights management (DRM) technology, developed exclusively by Portcullis MF Technologies for Bahoogle inc.

Individual content on pages can be discussed at water coolers once only. Any further use - or mention of the content - say at a bar or on the sofa - consitutes an infringement of the license agreement you agreed to by reading this book. If caught, you may be subject to criminal penalties and a 1000 years in jail.

Bugs
Every new revolutionary technology has a few teething troubles. This book is no exception. If your book crashes or if you discover a bug, please save us the trouble of having to track it down ourselves, by filling in a bug report form online at: www.theinternetnowinhandybookform.com. Yes, sorry for the inconvenience. No, you won't be paid.

TECHNICAL SUPPORT FREQUENTLY ASKED QUESTIONS

A page looks blank...
Have you tried closing then opening the book again?

The pages are stuck together!
Don surgical gloves and wipe with clean soapy sponge back and forth repeatedly until a soft soapy broth forms. Repeat, backwards and forwards, backwards and forwards, for five minutes or so. Ah yeah.

I'm not finding this book funny!
Aren't you? Remember: only unfunny people find things unfunny.

My book has a virus!
At time of writing (yesterday), there have been no known incidences of viruses on this book. So shut up. You're making it up..

Your book is not water resistant. Keep it dry. The moving parts may be damaged otherwise. Do not use harsh chemicals or industrial acid to clean your book. Wipe it with a soft cloth or a baby wipe. Or send us £10 to receive a handy anti-virus disinfectant wipe.

Care

Life's difficult enough without having to worry about the expense and hassle of replacing your book. So why not register your book with Bahoogle Care. Then if it gets lost, stolen or dropped off a cliff, or maliciously snatched out of your hands and shoved up into your colon, just send us the full cover price and we'll send you a replacement book of the same model absolutely free (excluding packaging and delivery) within 28 weeks.

Peace of mind!
Bahoogle Care covers you for: spills, dents, lending it out and then forgetting who you leant it to, toilet stains, dog eatings, cat maulings, hamster making nestings. All those.

Replacement
Yep, we'll replace your book. However replacement will not be provided where the loss or damage is caused by or consists of:
– normal wear or tear
– rusting
– confiscation by teachers or other authoritarian figures
– improper maintenance
– tearing, smearing, ripping, folding

Claiming Under Care
To speed up your claim please make a note of the key facts of the loss: the time, the date, where you lost it, what you were doing, why you were so bloody distracted, what the hell was so important that you took your eyes off it, how it got damaged, why it got damaged, why this is at least the second time you damaged something like this, why you never learn, why you always get things wrong, why your head is in the clouds, why you're never going to amount to anything if you keep pissing around like this, what steps you've taken to recover the book, the people you've spoken to, everyone you've spoken to, everyone you've spoken to ever, where you've hunted around, why you haven't said sorry, why it's me who's going to have to clear up this bloody mess as per bloody usual.

Care Tips
– Don't leave your book unattended in a public place
– Never lend your book to anyone else, even your best friends.
– Don't leave your book on public transport, such as buses, planes or trains.

Back Issues

Check out rare and collectible editions of this book from yesteryear. Yes. Yesteryear. And beyond then!

Many people are surprised when we say that we've been printing the Internet in a handy book form for nearly five decades. Piss off, they say. If they hang around, they are nearly always surprised to learn that the Internet has also been around for nearly five decades, in various forms. And that, whenever the internet has evolved, Bahoogle has evolved too, marrying the scope of the online world to the convenient portability of a paper-and-ink book. Or something. Here's a little girl.

The very first Internet in book form

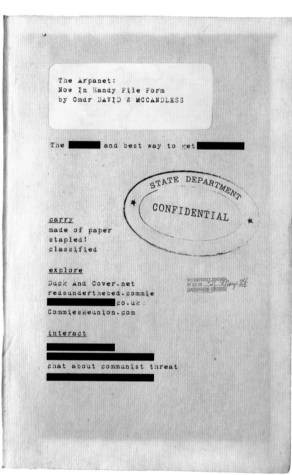

A chance to own this ultra rare first edition, recently declassified by the US government. Most of the content is illegible due to classification but still it remains an exciting porthole to a bygone age. And an expensive one. Perfect for the discerning spod, this collectors edition can be snapped up for a mere £55,000.

80s version

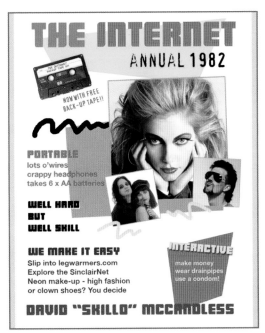

One of several yearly christmas "pop" editions printed during the decade that taste forgot. £25 each.

1974 Vintage Edition

This rare edition is tye-dyed on recycled Whole Earth paper. It mixes poetry and photocopied pictures of topless women. £99

Early 90s volumes 1-10

Before graphics. Before colour even. Before capitalists steamed in and stole the internet from us. Anyway, £400 for the lot anyone?

Late 90s

Mega indulgence and zero business plan. This 400 page edition, printed on silver, catches the spirit of the times. £120 million.

Buy Merchandise

Expand the experience of owning your favourite book . And become a walking advert for our brand. Everyone wins when you buy our merchandise

Branded Goods

The Internet: Now In Handy Book Form Toilet paper
Wipe your ass with it £4.99

The Internet: Now In Handy Book Form Pencil Case
Store pencils *and* pens. £9.99

The Internet: Now In Handy Book Form! Cock Pump
What is there to say? £39.99

Enhance your reading pleasure...

Deluxe Spellcheck £9.97

Bookmark Attachment Utilisation Dongles £14.99

SteadiRead™ Deluxe Hands Free £199.99

Visual Upgrades £98.99

STM Protective Neuro Sleeve Glove Bag £49.99

Vertical Storage Solutions from £119.99

Personal Privacy Shield £131.20

Perpendicular Vertical Access Precipators £39.99

Portable Protection Lock £110.99

Shopping Kart

Here is a list of items you have chosen to buy.

Item	Price:	Quantity

Your shopping basket is empty.

You don't seem to have bought anything.

Er....

Why do you think we made this book?

To entertain you??

Get back and order some stuff.

Proceed to checkout

Acknowledgements

Original Illustrations

16 Nauseating Optical Illusion **Peter Ayres;** 21 iRule: **Nik Roope / vi-r-us.com;** iTug: **Nik Roope / vi-r-us.com;** Mysteron: **Phil South / ideasdigital.com;** iMug: **Phil South /ideasdigital.com;** 22 Changing rooms **Peter Ayres;** How wear yours **Dean Kerrigan / cropdusters.co.uk;** 29 Impossible Chords **Delfina Bottesini;** Teletext **Phil South / ideasdigital.com;** 30 Aline **Simon Pegg / greatarchitect. wordpress.com;** 31 Laptop self-destruct **David Martin / Loveneon.com;** Blinkers **Alex Morris / VictoriaSpeedBoat.com;** 36 Phimosis & firkin **Alex Morris / VictorianSpeedBoat.com;** 43 Illustrations **Aegir Hallmundir / paperpixel.co.uk;** Metal gear chugger **Lee Sullivan / leesullivan.co.uk;** Pong2007 **Phil South / ideasdigital.com;** 45 Home Cosmetic Testing Kit **Doctor When / planetsimon.co.uk;** 51 Cajun Fried Lettuce **Rhodri Marsden / rhodri.biz;** 55 Hypochondriac Diagram **David Martin / loveneon.com;** 61 Atlas sphere **Alex Morris / VictorianSpeedBoat.com;** 62 House trap, Three Way **Elliot Elam / elliotelam.com;** 63 Abduction **Elliot Elam / elliotelam.com;** Internet Date **original concept John Comeau;** Painting Sudoku By Numbers **Alex Morris / VictorianSpeedBoat.com;**

65 Bolloxpedia Globe **Phil South / ideasdigital.com;** 69 Chinapedia Globe **Phil South / ideasdigital.com;** 70 Abode Kyotostop **Alex Morris / VictorianSpeedBoat.com;** Animated GIF Print Studio **Alex Morris / VictorianSpeedBoat.com;** ExcelAnt **Phil South / ideasdigital.com;** Mucrosoft Repeating Grey Grid **Phil South / ideasdigital.com;** 80 Tomb Raider ZX **Phil South / ideasdigital.com;** Gran Turismo ZX81 **Chris Ahchay;** Donkey Dong **Phil South / ideasdigital.com;** Quake 64 **Phil South / ideasdigital.com;** Tekken BSE **Phil South / ideasdigital.com;** Halflife NES **Schwenz;** Grand Theft Auto Text Adventure **original concept by Matt;** 81 Tim Berties Lee Diary **Peter Ayres;** 86 Lemon Diet **Mathemagician;** Kitten Diet **Neurozys;** 98 Glastzombie **Phil South / ideasdigital.com;** 100 Klabamm **HnlDesign / HnlDesign.nl;** 103 Bomb Recipe **Rhodri Marsden / Rhodri.biz;** 104 DP Nebula **Alex Morris / VictorianSpeedBoat.com;** 105 Cropcircles **Alex Morris / VictorianSpeedBoat.com;** 111 Squillion Dollar Page **Phil South / ideasdigital.com;** 112 Hat Or Not **Rhodri Marsden / Rhodri.biz;** 114 Erotically Charged Stapler **Rhodri Marsden / Rhodri.biz;** 119 Zombies **Phil South / ideasdigital.com;** 125 PCP **BilboBarneyBobs / bilbobarneybobs.co.uk;**

Photo Credits

All photos listed are from istockphoto.com Credits in the following format: username / real name (when available)

cover Nerd **lugo;** Babe **phildate;** Biz guy **icongenic;** 006 Baby reading **snapphoto;** 008 Pill cocktail **tobntno / Gunther Beck;** Toad **pasterscott / Scott Leigh;** Smoker **annedde;** Doughnut **diane39 / Diane Diederich;** Married couple **trenchardj / Jennifer Trenchard;** Widow **Kalisratova / Elena Kalistratova;** Cat **zimmytws;** Whispering girls **MsSponge / Karen Town;** 010 CEO **gocosmonaut;** Darren&Emma **trenchardj / Jennifer Trenchard;** Tokyo Ritz **poba / Gregor Hoevar;** BloodyWomen **simonmcconico;** 011 Writer **hidesy / Amanda Rohde;** Mark&Sue **tobkatrina / Katrina Brown;** Hassel DavidOff **caracterdesign / Eva Serrabassa;** 016 Woman **iahulbak;** Meat **T_BEANS;** Hitched **hidsey Amanda Rohde;** Pregnancy Test **Martin-Carlsson / Martin Carlsson;** Half House **heyoka / Petra Kukofka;** Aerial Stadium **FreezingTime / Teun van den Dries;** 017 Mosque **rzdeb / Rafal Zdeb;** Tudor houses **moonmeister / David Woods;** Refugees **starfotograf;** Lake **sundown001 / Randy Mayes;** Alien **LPETTET / Lee Pettet;** 019 Virus **Eraxion / Sebastian Kaulitzki;** 021 Ibuprofen

Grafissimo; Sleeping man **Brainsil / Silvia Boratti;** Bok **brm1949 / Bruce MacQueen;** 022 Scared man **joshblake / Joshua Blake;** Wow group **joshblake / Joshua Blake;** Leaping woman **binabina / roberta casaliggi;** Yeah! Man **myfault1 / Jeff Edney;** 023 Darren & Emma **trenchardj / Jennifer Trenchard;** Shields **photosmash / Leif Norman;** Leaping man **diego_cervo / diego cervo;** Drunk **PhotoEuphoria / Jaimie Duplass;** 024 No to drugs **falcatraz / Ryan KC Wong;** Smoker **annedde;** Confidex **tstajduhar / Tomislav Stajduhar;** 025 Unhappy couple 1 **phfft / Nuno Silva;** Unhappy couple 2 **coloroftime / Cristian Ardelean;** 026 Toohott **caracterdesign / Eva Serrabassa;** Writer **hidesy / Amanda Rohde;** 027 Widow **Kalisratova / Elena Kalistratova;** Grave **ImagineGolf / Andrew Penner;** Girl **Laartist / Rebecca Ellis;** 028 Dreamcatcher **sangfoto / Sang Nguyen;** Writer **hidesy / Amanda Rohde;** Ceo **gocosmonaut;** Justbyou cake-eater **drduey / Duard van der Westhuizen;** 029 Fellatrix **yoglimogli / Odelia Cohen;** Bill Bison: **Toby Slater;** 030 Red car **h0rde / James Rodkey;** Soldier doll **robynmac / Robyn MacKenzie;** Monster doll **mwookie / Peter Galbraith;** Superhero doll **emyerson / Ethan Myerson;** Perfume bottles: **ronen, studioraminta, bokeyphoto;** 031 Kite **Viorika / Viorika Prikhodko;**

Fat guy **myfault1 / Jeff Edney;** Fur jacket guy **upheaval / Jeremiah Deasey;** 034-035 Real life pic **beright / Kristin Smith;** 036 Deepest africa **ogen / Ogen Perry;** Build a pub **eye joy / Bonnie Schupp;** Mr pub **simonox / Simon Oxley;** 037 Front room **EricVega / M Eric Honeycutt;** Worcester mews **Jaap2;** Pernineum **dkapp12 / Denise Kappa;** Pudenda crescent **JPSchrage / Jan Paul Schrage;** Everygreen sq **Veni / Jeremy Edwards;** Vainglorious passage **vicnt / victor zastol skiy;** Monkey hutch **jbreeves / Brent Reeves;** Jizz sluice **Terraxplorer;** Half house **heyoka / Petra Kukofka;** Arnsdale way **upsidedowndog / Niilo Tippler;** Roller **kingvald;** Win! win! win! **snapphoto / Leigh Schindler;** Lofty ambitions **Hofpils / Heiko Etzrodt;** 039-040 Tokyo Ritz **poba** / Gregor Hoevar; New Age Scientist **frenchmen77 / Tyler Boyes;** 041 Greenland **ersier / Ersler Dmitry;** Fries **khz / bora ucak;** Tomatoes **Suzifoo / Suzannah Skelton, ranplett, kcline / Kelly Cline;** Candy **sangfoto / Sang Nguyen;** Cork **alaincouillaud;** Swimmers: **proxyminder;** 042 Shotputter **pacifica / Daniel Berman;** Tennis player **frankysze / Franky Sze;** DIY Disaster **GreenPimp / Tom Young;** Motor racing **HHakim / Hazlan Abdul Hakim;** Svargoord **myfault1 / Jeff Edney;** Rugby **suemack / Sue McDonald;** F1 **afby71 / Ahmad Faizal**

Yahya; McGinty **robh;** 044 Allaboutyou **jsmith / Jeffrey Smith;** Pinkshit **FONG_KWONG_CHO / Dave Cho;** Shampoo special **jhorrocks / Justin Horrocks;** Pornforgirls **dtseller / Dustin Steller;** Chicken **gmnicholas / Greg Nicholas;** Mens toilets **peeterv / Peeter Viisimaa;** Diet **gvictoria / Graca Victoria;** Interiors **kash76 / Alexey Kashin;** Shopping **simonkr / Simon Kri;** Self-help **yoepro / Jonas Engstrom;** Love&sex **aldra;** Scratchcards **Gerville / Gerville Hall;** Beauty **iconogenic / Kateryna Govorushchenko;** Poker **shaunt / Shaun Lowe;** Desperate housewives **bobbieo / Robert Osbourne;** Total body makeover **Steve 'Buzz' Pearce;** Tampod **laartist / Rebecca Ellis;** Photoshop **marti157900 / Lori Martin;** Self pinching bottom **casarsa / Valentin Casarsa;** Self pinching claw **inok / Konstantin Inozemtsev;** 045 Aurox **aldra;** Facemask **jhorrocks / Justin Horrocks;** Legwarmers **tomazl / Tomaz Levstek;** Stilts **phfft / Nuna Silva;** Glow gums **dem10 / Emrah Turudu;** Slapheads **CO_2 / Harmen Piekema;** Affirmations **blackred;** Emergency **casarsa / Valentin Casarsa;** Anti-diet diet **diane39 / Diane Diederich;** Bloody laughing **hidsey / Amanda Rohde;** Suddenly **LDF / Luca di Filippo;** Cold dark stranger **milosluz / Milos Luzanin;** 046 iPirate **nspimages / Nicholas Sutcliffe;** Doctor **nano /**

Nancy Louie; Feet **benoitb / Benoit Beauregard;** Cross **dra_schwartz / Andrei Tchernov;** 048 Bored Pilots, Mixed Messages, Blowjob Competition **Freezingtime / Teun Van Den Dries;** The Jaws Of Death **slobo / Slobo Mitic;** 049 Action Movie **Freezingtime / Teun van den Dries;** Hard Drivin' **slovbo / Slobo Mitic;** Deliberate Mistake **Freezingtime / Teun van den Dries;** 050 Girl with laptop **aldra;** Fistful of dollars **road-warrior / david bronson glover;** Raining money **kativ;** Red Car **h0rde / James Rodkey;** Volcano **jgroup / james steidl;** Battleship **bergmannD / Dean Bergmann;** 051 Grimdust Feeling Crap **Miles Tudor;** Carrot **UteHil;** Spray **Millanovic;** Meats **terrasprite;** 052 Bill Bison **hsandler / Howard Sandler;** 054 Drug cocktail **tobntno / Gunther Beck;** Doctor **nano / Nancy Louie;** Gloves **danielle71 / Dana Spiropoulou;** Head **angelhell;** Hypochondriac **pixelbrat / Amy Walter;** Hemorrhoids **theprint / Rasmus Rasmussen;** Rash **abdone;** 055 Candy background **nico_blue / Nicholas Monu;** 056 Jumping couple **lisegagne / Lise Gagne;** Work for the man **sjlocke / Sean Locke;** Stationery thief **peeterv / Peeter Viisimaa;** Arms deal **sdominick / Sharon Dominick;** Teat team **jirivondracek / Jiri Vondracek;** Polish flash builder **gocrawford / Bill Crawford;** Resume **tacojim / Jim Jurica;** 058-059 Bully **lisafx / Lisa F. Young;**

Shadow **puncher mandygodbehear;** 80s girl **lisegagne / Lise Gagne;** Goths **sdominick / Sharon Dominick;** Cassette **bns124 / Neil Sullivan;** George michael-alike **uniball / Pete Collins;** 060 Family **tobkatrina / Katrina Brown;** Nappy **Renphoto / Renee Lee;** Spillage **Stalman / Tyler Stalman;** Bruise **wekiwis / Colin Stitt;** Pregnancy **sunara / Susanna Fieramosca Naranja;** Tough Parent **pjjones;** Calendar **ferrantraite / Ferran Traite Solen;** 061 Trunk **PKM1 / Paul Mckeown;** Crying child **perkmeup / Thomas Perkins;** Cyclops 9000 **Alisonlarge / Alison Large;** Baby Jesus XL **olio / Peggy Chen;** Mobile Phone **alicat / Alice Millikan;** 062 Cocaine & razor blade **kickers / Christoph Ermel;** Dice **liftconcepts / Ben Thomas;** 063 Fat naked body **mariusFM77 / Florea Marius Catalin;** Girl body **lisafx / Lisa F.Young;** 064 Ring **humonia / Monika Wisniewska;** Elf Princes **fmbackx / Famke Backx;** 065 Church **JillianPond / Jillian Pond;** 066 Hassel Davidoff pictures **caracterdesign / Eva Serrabassa;** 067 Buddha **april30 / Auke Holwerda;** 068 4x4 **shaunl / Shaun Lowe;** Seafood **4x4;** Stressed man **ZlatKOstic / Zlatko Kostic;** Fishing Boat **sethakan / Hakan Karlsson;** Flower **mbbirdy / Matjaz Boncina;** 069 China **slydeproductions / Stuart Dunn;** 070 Teen boy **photobuff / Susan Stevenson;** Teen girl

Chainsaw **Guy Kirza / Kirill Zdorov;** Alien **LPETTET / Lee Pettet;** RIP stone **ToddSm66 / Todd Smith;** Big Zombie **Vasko / Vasko Miokovic;** Scared Girl **theprint / Rasmus Rasmussen;** Cockzilla **Spanishalex / Alex Bramwell;** Tiny man **joshblake / Joshua Blake;** Cockness **Monster Matt84 / Matt Craven;** Phantom **caracterdesign / eva serrabassa;** Knife Girl **dolgachov / Lev Dolgatshjov;** Lightning Soubrette; 119 auto-erotic tragedy **yew / Edyta Cholcha-Cisowska;** rent boys **GoGo;** paying money **sleddogtwo / Dennis Hoyne;** surgeon **fmatte / Falko Matte;** deep throat **rtracewell / Rick Tracewell;** proctologist **creacart;** mechanic **anouchka / Anna Bryukhanova;** plumbers **alaistaircotton / Alistair Cotton;** plumbers cleft **BrainOnAShelf;** hiphop hands **upheaval / Jeremiah Deasey;** pink limo

texasmary 121 Book **rocknrollfun / Laura Tomlinson;** 124 Ketamine sunset **Flappers / Warren Lindsay;** Coffee cup **JLGutierrez / José Luis Gutiérrez;** Hamper **princessdlaf / Nina Shannon;** Atm pattern **kirstypargeter / kirsty pargeter;** Titanium hooter **a-papantoniou / Antonis Papantoniou;** 126 Vampyre Queen **caracterdesign / eva serrabassa;** Bat **justbobf / Bob Faulkner;** Mountain **wingmar / Ingmar Wesemann;** Guru **DanielHalePhoto / Daniel Hale;** Grief **efenzi / Maciej Laska;** Pincochet **duncan1890 / Duncan Walker;** GiftBox **kcline / Kelly Cline;** 127 Cat **zimmytws;** Barbed Wire **ArtisRams / Artis Rams;** House **BCFC / Paul Hill;** Noose **freshpix / Maxim Sergienko;** Ballerina **Alija;** Religious **trenchardj / Jennifer Trenchard;** Atheist **Breigouze / Patrick Breig;** Cuckold **hidesy / Amanda**

Rohde; 128 Mummy **joshblake / Joshua Blake;** Dog **wig walik;** Ballerina **Alija;** Sausages **sburel / Sebastien Burel;** Kidney **PaulCowan / Paul Cowan;** Warriors **Gerville / Gerville Hall;** Toilet head **Joss / Jostein Hauge;** 129 Helicopter **sierrarat / Ken Babione;** White House **slang78 / Pietro Valdinoci;** Iran **rzdeb / Rafal Zdeb;** Algae **JamieWilson / Jamie Wilson;** National Guard **kramer-1 / stephen mulcahey;** Fencing **ftwitty / Frances Twitty;** Car On Fire **Olas / Nicholas Burke;** USA **jsnyderdesign / Jim Snyder;** 132 Woman **Anjark / Jaroslaw Grubba;** Man **sjlocke / Sean Locke;** 133 Clipboard woman **Trigrey / Dmitry Obukhov;** 134-135 Girl **caracterdesign / Eva Serrabassa;** 60s pamphlet **claylib / Clayton Hansen;** Cassette **bns124 / Neil Sullivan;** 80s Girl **lisegagne / Lise Gagne;** Goths **sdominick / Sharon Dominick;** George Michael

uniball / Pete Collins; 70s Pattern **Artzone / John Rawsterne;** Moustache Guy **Elerium / Dane Wirtzfeld;** Wow Girl **caracterdesign / eva serrabassa;** Sunglasses Guy **InkkStudios / Kris Hanke;** Slides **ranplett;** Cartoon Girl **Maljuk / Olena Patsyuk;** 136 Toilet Paper **tainted / tanya c;** Water Pump **DaddyBit;** Dictionary **tacojim / Jim Jurica;** Paperclips **arekmalang / Suprijono Suharjoto;** Pulpit **digitalhallway / Reuben Schulz;** Glasses **ajsn / Antonio Nunes;** Plastic Bag **kencameron / Ken Cameron;** Bookcases **TalonDI / Sherrianne Talon;** Hood **caracterdesign / eva serrabassa;** Bookends **peterspiro / Peter Spiro;** Vice **LongHa2006 / Long Ha;** monkey hutch **jbreeves / Brent Reeves;** Darren & Emma **trenchardj / Jennifer Trenchard;** Thumb Woman **phildate / Phil Date.**

Contributors' websites

BilboBarneyBobs / bilbobarneybobs.co.uk
Elliot Elam / elliotelam.com
Piers Gibbon / piersgibbon.com
Aegir Hallmundir / paperpixel.co.uk
HnlDesign / HnlDesign.nl
Dean Kerrigan / cropdusters.co.uk
Anne Marie-Payne / ampnet.co.uk
Rhodri Marsden / rhodri.biz
David Martin / Loveneon.com
Alex Morris / VictoriaSpeedBoat.com
Simon Pegg / greatarchitect. wordpress.com
Nik Roope / vi-r-us.com

Toby Slater / tobyslater.com
Phil South / ideasdigital.com
Lee Sullivan / leesullivan.co.uk
Iain Tait / crackunit.com
Dave Walker / cartoonchurch.com
Doctor When / planetsimon.co.uk

Be wowed
by our website

Did you enjoy your internet book experience? Want more? Then visit the 'online' version of this web book...

Top child technicians from developing nations have worked day and night to rework these high-resolution pages into a lower-quality 'electronic internet' form. View it today at:

http://www.TheInternetNowInHandyBookForm.com

It's chock full of great things:
- all your favourite book websites
- additional content
- a cool-sounding members club that's a thinly veiled excuse to get your email address into
- our database forever
plus!
no end of adverts, banners, popups, adlines, cut-ins, dynamic dropdowns, inserters, tower blocks, liftoffs, skypullers, and adverts spinning around on lasers

Visit it today!

```
<!DOCTYPE btml PUBLIC "-//W3C//DTD BHTML 1.0 Transitional//EN/Blah Blah Who came up this stuff?"
"http://www.pageturntechnologies.com/TR/bhtml1/">
<head>
<body>
<legs>
<trunk>
<neck>
<title>The Internet Now In Handy Book Form!</title>
<meta http-equiv="Content-Type" content="text/html; charset=ISO-8859-1" />
<meta name="description" content="a funny spoof book of the internet, well that's what the idea
was">
<meta name="keywords" content="bad jokes, phimosis, scaries, baby swans, buttery breasts, smug
Schmapple users, jokes, wedding nerds, drug hypocrites, dating scaries, stapled stomachs, dollies
for men, male humiliation, dreary repetitive bloggers, life, dark pubs, materialism, angela from
arabia, mentos eating kittens driving monster trucks, the world is screwed!, sport injuries,
female vanity, dying to industrial beats, bedroom musicians, blowjob competitions, mr mgayi,
powdered mineral water, bill bison, self-indulgent writers, hypochondriacs, soulless corporate
hamster wheels, school reunion sites, smug parents, callous sexual experimenteers, sexual elves
issues, online encyclopedia pedants, smug libertarian journalists, fascistic governments, kak,
boring bloggers, diet fads, social networking scaries, police, america, the whole culture, banal
gossips, spods, pre-conventional worldviews, my ass, and me disappearing fast up it, crap porn,
irritable fridges, middle class wankers, drug culture, fundies, atheists and spods who write
books like these.">
<meta name="Identifier-URL" content="http://www.theinternetnowinhandybookform.com">
<meta name="ROBOTS" content'"RULE">
<link href="backcover/css/tinihbf.css" rel="stylesheet">
.me {
  height: 6ft;
  weight: medium;
  width: medium;
  color: #ffffff;
  padding-bottom: normal, ok?;
  ego-size: 8;
  family: mad, crazy, doolally;
  class="lower middle"
}
.thisbook  {
  padding-front: 12 pages;
  padding-back: 6 pages;
  content: okay;
  joke-spacing: 90ems;
  margin: slim;
  margin-agent: 15%;
}
.america {
  border-bottom: 10 miles;
  border-bottom-style: strong;
  border-left: strong;
  border-left-style: watery;
  border-right: strong;
  border-top: weak;
  border-top-style: dotted;
  }
</head>
<table width="98%" colour="brown" legs="4" stains="1">
<remember>to get james to give it a wipe</remember>
<10 print>This Book is Skill</print>
<goto 10>
<nads>wrong language, wrong century</nads>

<br><ok><en><life>
<type="this code" all=day>

</table>
</legs>
</trunk>
</neck>
</body>
</html>
```